DSP Consulting

BUSINESS
BY
REFERRAL

A Sure-Fire Way to
Generate New Business

Business
by
Referral

A Sure-Fire Way to

Generate New Business

BY

Ivan R. Misner, Ph.D.

AND

Robert Davis

Bard Press

Austin, Texas

BUSINESS BY REFERRAL

A Sure-Fire Way to Generate New Business

Printed in Canada by Webcom Limited.

Permission to reproduce or transmit in any form or by any means, electronic or mechanical, including photocopying and recording, or by an information storage and retrieval system, must be obtained by writing to the publisher at the address below.

Bard Press
5275 McCormick Mtn. Dr.
Austin, Texas 78734
512-266-2112, fax 512-266-2749
ray@bardpress.com

Visit our web site at www.bardpress.com.

A Paradigm Publishing Book.

To order the book, contact your local bookstore or call 800-688-9394.

ISBN 1-885167-27-X trade paperback

Library of Congress Cataloging-in-Publication Data
Misner, Ivan R., 1956-
    Business by referral : a sure-fire way to generate new business / by
Ivan R. Misner and Robert Davis.
       p.   cm.
    Includes index.
    ISBN 1-885167-28-8 (hardcover), -- ISBN 1-885167-27-X (pbk.)
    1. Marketing--Management. 2. Business referrals. I. Davis, Robert, 1955-   . II. Title.
HF5415. 13.M544   1997
658.8--DC21

97-41046
CIP

The authors may be contacted at the following addresses:

Ivan R. Misner, Ph.D.
BNI Enterprises Inc.
545 College Commerce Way
Upland, CA 91786-4377
800-825-8286 (outside So. California)
909-608-7575, fax 909-608-7676
misner@bni.com

Robert Davis
Robert Davis Associates
11688 Range View Rd.
Mira Loma, CA 91752
909-681-0686, fax 909-681-1924
RDavisNSA@aol.com

CREDITS
Developmental editing: Jeff Morris
Editing: Kathy Bork
Copyediting: Deborah Costenbader
Proofreading: Doreen Piano
Indexing: Linda Webster
Project management/text design/production: Jeff Morris
Jacket design: Hugh Pirnie, Pirnie Marketing

First printing: Nov. 1997
Second printing: Feb. 1998

Third printing: Feb. 2003
Fourth printing: Aug. 2004

DEDICATION

*In life, some people see in us the possibilities
that we do not see in ourselves. I dedicate this
book to three high-school teachers who did that
for me. To Frank Rogers, Art Hiett, and
Frank Romero: You made a difference.*

— Ivan R. Misner, Ph.D

*To the late Cavett Robert, CSP, CPAE,
founder of the National Speakers Association.*

— Robert Davis

CONTENTS

●

ACKNOWLEDGMENTS

We wish to thank the many people who provided valuable input, insights, and feedback on our manuscript, including Candace Bailly, Ken Braly, Craig Campana, Virginia Devine, Daniel Diener, Jeannie Esposito, Connie Hinton, Gene Holiman, Sheryl Horton, Jackee McNitt, Shelli Prochaska, Judy Sherkow, Gene Siciliano, Jan Triplett, and Pat Woy.

We would also like to thank the thousands of business professionals (many of whom were members of BNI and NSA) who took their time to complete the referral survey that inspired the creation of this book.

As always, a big thank you is due for the editing, suggestions, and support of Elisabeth Misner, who has provided valuable comments and recommendations on the manuscript. We also thank Belinda Davis, Adhana Davis, and Willie Boyette for their ongoing support.

We would like to recognize the special efforts of Ray Bard and his staff at Bard Press for their expertise and commitment; they are truly a pleasure to work with. Finally, we would like to thank Jeff Morris, whose substantial assistance on this project made it possible.

ABOUT THE AUTHORS

Dr. Ivan R. Misner is the founder and president of Business Network Int'l., the world's largest networking service organization, in San Dimas, California. Internationally recognized as networking's guru, Dr. Misner is a motivational keynote speaker for major corporations and associations throughout North America. He has been featured in the *Wall Street Journal, Los Angeles Times, New York Times, Entrepreneur* magazine, and on television and radio shows from coast to coast.

Dr. Misner earned his doctorate at the University of Southern California, specializing in organizational development. His doctoral dissertation was on business development networks, and he has published many books, articles, and tapes on management and networking, including the bestselling *The World's Best Known Marketing Secret.*

Dr. Misner is on the business administration faculty at Cal Poly University, Pomona, and is in *Who's Who of Leading American Executives.* He is on the board of directors for the LeRoy Haynes Center, a nonprofit program for abused and neglected children. He has been nominated twice for *Inc.* magazine's "Entrepreneur of the Year" award.

Dr. Misner resides in La Verne, California, with his wife, Elisabeth, and three children, Ashley, Cassie, and Trey.

Robert Davis is a respected author, motivational keynote speaker, and trainer. He is author of *Implement Now, Perfect Later: 52 Practical Ways to Increase Gains and Decrease Pains of Perfectionism.* He is often asked to speak on perfectionism, achieving goals, generating referrals, and building rewarding professional relationships.

Mr. Davis is a member of the 1998–99 National Speakers Association (NSA) leadership team and vice president of the Greater Los Angeles Chapter of NSA. He is a former consultant for Drake Beam Morin, the world's leading career transition management organization. He has over eighteen years of experience in human resources management, including employment, employee relations, organization development, and training.

Mr. Davis is a member of the Business & Professional Development Institute Advisory Committee. He was the cofounder and executive director of the Small Business Network. He received his master's degree from the University of San Francisco and his bachelor's degree from Pomona College.

Mr. Davis resides in Mira Loma, California, with his wife, Belinda, and daughter, Adhana.

Part

I

An Old "New" Way of Doing Business

Part	Chapter	Referral Marketing Plan Component	
I	**1**		
	2		
II	**3**	1. Mission Statement	41
	4	2. Products and Services	42
	5	3. Target Market	43
III	**6**	4. Competition	45
	7		
	8		
	9		
	10		
IV	**11**	5. Matching Needs and Prospective Sources	93
	12	6. Tactics	115
V	**13**		
	14	7. Referral Marketing System	123, 132, 144
	15		
	16	8. Time Budget	149
	17	9. Calendar	152
VI	**18**	10. Cost Budget	154
	19	11. Sales and Referral Projections	160
	20	12. Tracking and Evaluation	171

Chapter 1

A Cure for the Common Cold Call

*Rediscovering
the Rewards of
Referral Marketing*

IMAGINE THAT YOUR HOUSE has been damaged by a hailstorm and your roof needs repairs. Who do you call? You've never hired a building contractor before, so you look in the Yellow Pages and find A. A. Aaron Construction Company; twenty years in business, says the ad. Because the storm hit so many houses, though, Aaron can't get to you for at least two months. You try two or three more roofers, with similar results.

You know it's going to rain again over the next few weeks, so you're desperate. You check the paper. It's full of ads for roofing contractors you've never heard of. You phone one who calls himself Zippy Zeke; he wants cash up front. Is he bonded? Yeah, yeah, no sweat. You tell Zeke you'll call back.

Things are looking bleak. You wonder what your friend Jerry would do in this situation. You call him. Jerry says his sister Sherry had her house completely remodeled two years ago and liked the job.

You call Sherry. Sherry says Modine's Modular Materials built a new room on her house. She tells you the roof they put on is even better than the original. She's okay with the price, too.

You call Modine. Modine says he's pretty busy but he's got everybody working overtime and can probably get started next week. His price is a little higher than you expected, but you don't mind because you feel sure he'll do a good job. You ask why he isn't in the Yellow Pages. He is, he says, but it's not a display ad. He does a little print and radio advertising, too, but he gets almost all the business he can handle by word of mouth.

Calls like these are made millions of times a day. When they need a financial planner, a chiropractor, a lawyer, or almost any other professional, most people would rather hire someone who's done business with someone they know. Most of us want some assurance, besides the vendor's own advertising claims, that we will get our money's worth. We want to find a business we can trust.

SELF-TORTURE BY COLD CALL

NOW LET'S LOOK at another kind of buyer-seller transaction, this time from the seller's point of view. Let's suppose that, like most businesspeople, you rely on either mass advertising or targeted marketing campaigns to get your business name in front of large numbers of potential customers — to stir up some name recognition. You will, of course, generate a certain amount of business and, at the same time, attract people who want a product you don't carry or a service you don't perform.

Like many of your colleagues, you decide to go active rather than passive. You get long lists of people or businesses who might (or might not) be interested in what you offer. You begin cold calling them. Here's how it goes:

"Ace Janitorial Services, Supply Division, Ms. Gargle's office. Can I help you?"

"This is Bob White of Zenith Cleaning Products. May I speak with Ms. Gargle?"

"I'll see if she's in. Will you hold, please?" (Several minutes of elevator music interrupted by Ace commercials.)

"Ace Janitorial Services, Supply Division, Ms. Gargle's office. Can I help you?"

"Yes, I'm holding for Ms. Gargle."

"Oh, yes, is this Mr. White?"

"Yes, it is."

"Mr. White, I'm sorry, but it looks like Ms. Gargle has stepped out of her office."

"Do you know when she'll be back?"

"I'm sorry, I don't."

"Then could I speak with her assistant?"

"That would be Mr. Hyde. Please hold, I'll transfer your call." (A long series of clicks, followed by several minutes of elevator music and Ace commercials.)

"Supply, Mr. Hyde's office."

"May I speak with Mr. Hyde, please?"

"Who may I say is calling?"

"This is Mr. White of Zenith Cleaning Products."

"Please hold." (Two clicks and a commercial fragment.)

"This is Hyde."

"Yes, my name is Bob White and I represent Zenith Cleaning Products. I wonder if I might — "

"Bob, I should tell you up front that we've been doing business with Astonishing Chemicals for many years and we're pretty satisfied with their stuff."

"I'm sure that's true, Mr. Hyde, but I can show you a totally new kind of cleaning system that works better and costs less — "

"Hey, I'd love to hear about it, but I'm late for a meeting, so why don't you pop something in the mail and let me read about it. Okay? Thanks."

How does cold calling make you feel? Pretty lousy, right? You end up with a knot in your stomach, a sore ear, a compound fracture of the ego, and very little to show for it. You can't really blame the people you call, either. They don't know anything about you. Are your products any good? Do you perform as advertised? Is your price right? Can you be trusted?

In other words, it's what — and who — they don't know that can hurt you.

EVERYBODY LIKES REFERRALS

ERE'S A FACT that most people in business today are well aware of: it's much better to do business with people who trust you. The referred lead is typically a much better prospect than someone you've never met or spoken with before, someone with whom you have nothing or no one in common. The referred prospect, experienced business professionals agree,

- is easier to close,
- has far fewer complaints,
- is more loyal,
- remains a client longer, and
- is more trusting.

Business professionals also like referrals because they bring in customers at little or no cost. Cold calling, which almost everyone hates, wastes an enormous amount of time for the few sales it eventually closes. Advertising, even when narrowly focused on specific markets, is relatively inefficient. But a single referral can bring in a chain reaction of business, as one satisfied customer tells others, who in turn tell still others.

Perhaps the best thing about referrals is that they bring in customers with a positive attitude.

Perhaps the best thing about referrals is that they bring in customers with a positive attitude, customers who trust the business because they believe their friends or business associates. Business transactions are easier to close because skeptics are usually screened out automatically by the person giving the referral.

More Referrals, Please

T HOUSANDS OF BUSINESS PROFESSIONALS have told us over the years that referrals are the most reliable, most rewarding, least expensive way of rounding up business. But we've found out something else: these same businesspeople feel they aren't getting enough referrals.

This is puzzling. If referrals are by far professionals' favorite way of finding business, what's stopping them from cultivating all the referrals they can handle? We decided to conduct a survey of our own.

Over six months we polled 2,350 businesspeople in the United States, Canada, Puerto Rico, and the United Kingdom — salespeople for large and small companies, small-business owners, and various professionals in both retail and service industries. We asked them to rate the effectiveness of various means of generating referrals, as well as what percentage of their business they were getting through referrals and what percentage they thought they should be getting.

The survey is brief and simple, but very revealing (see sidebar). Before you read any further, we'd like you to answer the questions yourself, then compare your responses with those of our respondents.

Here's what our survey showed about rounding up business through referrals. Most of our respondents consider networking groups, oral requests, and written requests their most effective means of generating referrals. Although their responses support what we have

Referrals Survey

1. What percentage of your business are you now getting through referrals?
   - ☐ Less than 10%   ☐ 51–60%
   - ☐ 11–20%   ☐ 61–70%
   - ☐ 21–30%   ☐ 71–80%
   - ☐ 31–40%   ☐ 81–90%
   - ☐ 41–50%   ☐ 91–100%

2. What percentage of your business would you realistically like to get through referrals?
   - ☐ Less than 10%   ☐ 51–60%
   - ☐ 11–20%   ☐ 61–70%
   - ☐ 21–30%   ☐ 71–80%
   - ☐ 31–40%   ☐ 81–90%
   - ☐ 41–50%   ☐ 91–100%

3. Check off all of the most effective methods that you are currently using to generate referrals:
   - ☐ Asking orally
   - ☐ Asking in writing (newsletters, referral forms, letters, etc.)
   - ☐ Participating in networking groups
   - ☐ Holding seminars or conducting speaking engagements
   - ☐ Existing customers do it without any prompting
   - ☐ Using the Internet or a computer bulletin board service (Prodigy, CompuServe, America Online, etc.)
   - ☐ Offering incentives to those who refer me (discounts, gifts, finder's fees, etc.)
   - ☐ Recognition of customers/clients/patients (thank you's in newsletter, posting on an in-house bulletin board, etc.)
   - ☐ Subscribe to a referral service (i.e., 1-800-DENTIST)
   - ☐ Other (please state what):
   - ☐ Other (please state what):
   - ☐ Other (please state what):

4. Do you use a systematic program of some kind to generate referrals? Systematic is defined as steps that you consistently apply to generate business referrals.
   - ☐ Yes   ☐ No

21

been saying for years — that networking groups pay off handsomely in terms of referral business — only 45 percent of our respondents actually use what they consider a systematic referral system.

Referrals from Networking Groups

The fact that over four out of five respondents recognize the value of networking groups suggests that most of them belong to one or more groups. In *The World's Best Known Marketing Secret: Building Your Business with Word-of-Mouth Marketing*, Ivan describes several types of networking groups that are commonly used to generate business referrals:

- Casual-contact networks — general business groups such as chambers of commerce that allow many people from various overlapping professions;
- Strong-contact networks — groups that allow only one member per profession and that meet weekly expressly to exchange leads;
- Community-service clubs — groups like Rotary and Kiwanis, which exist primarily to serve the community but which also are a good source of referrals;
- Professional associations — groups of people in a single industry or profession, whose primary purpose is to exchange information and ideas;
- Social/business groups — dual-purpose organizations such as the Jaycees that combine business and pleasure, sometimes with emphasis on the latter;
- Women's business organizations — relatively recent networking groups paralleling the "old-boy networks" that formerly excluded females.

The World's Best Known Marketing Secret also discusses the importance of diversifying the organizations that you participate in. If you're serious about generating business through referrals, no single group or type of networking organization will serve all your needs. Being a member of one group or type of group is not a guarantee of success. The best strategy is to select a well-rounded mix of organizations and to join or attend no two of the same type. This strategy also applies to speaking before groups and conducting seminars.

Referrals from Other Sources

Most successful sales training programs recommend that you not simply wait for referrals to come in on their own but that you ask for them. Our respondents did recognize the value of requesting referrals orally or in writing. It is important to understand, though, that there are many other ways, both direct and indirect, to solicit referrals. A systematic referral system incorporates most or all of these methods, as appropriate to your business or organization, to bring you a steady stream of referrals from diverse sources.

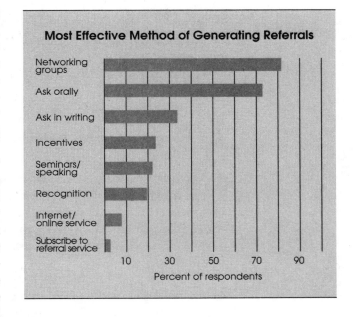

Who do you know who . . . ? One of the most efficient ways to get information about potential leads is the "Who do you know who . . . ?" approach, which Mark Sheer describes in *Referrals*. The use of this phrase in both oral and written communications, and in precisely this form, has proven effective in generating leads. Its open-ended form, inviting the listener to suggest names, is superior to a question that asks for only a yes or no answer, such as "Do you know anybody who . . . ?"

Incentives. It is important to give a prospective referral source some incentive for sending referrals your way. Incentives can range from simple recognition (an oral thank you, an awards ceremony before a group) to monetary rewards based on business generated. Nearly a quarter of our respondents consider incentives by themselves an effective generator of referrals.

Online networking. One new and rapidly growing source of referrals is online networking, especially via the Internet. In *Megatrends*, John Naisbitt argues that the more our technology tends to isolate us, the more we try to reach out, including through technology, to communicate. Although nothing can replace face-to-face contact, the Internet is becoming the most immediate and democratic manifestation of Naisbitt's prediction. It is a natural medium for word-of-mouth information about products and services. If it can keep its "people's network" feel as it grows — online veterans are militantly opposed to mass advertising on the Internet — it may greatly increase its usefulness in attracting referrals.

Referral services. Subscribing to a referral service was rated effective by only a small fraction of our respondents. This is not surprising. Most referral services are little more than paid advertising on demand, requiring the potential customer to take the initiative in searching out a needed product or service. Your prospect has no more reason to believe your referral service advertisement than if he heard it on the radio.

THE REFERRAL GAP REVEALED

A S WE ANALYZED the results of our survey, we noticed that, although most respondents recognize the value of referrals and the various methods of generating them, most get less than half their business through referrals. About five out of six would prefer to get much more. This is not too surprising, given the low cost and efficacy of referral marketing.

We refer to the difference between the two measures — percentage of business now being generated by referrals and percentage desired — as the "referral gap." The average business professional in the survey feels that there is a 30 to 40 percent gap between the amount of business being brought in through referrals and what she thinks she should be getting. Given the level of importance that people assign to the value of referral business, this is a huge gap.

The average business professional in the survey feels that there is a 30 to 40 percent gap between the amount of business being brought in through referrals and what she thinks she should be getting.

Why such a large discrepancy between the number of referrals desired and the number realized? This survey and our many years of experience working with business professionals, owners, and salespeople suggest that it is because few businesspeople plan or conduct a systematic marketing campaign to generate referrals.

Part of the reason for this deficiency is that our business schools are not teaching the next generation of business professionals the importance of referrals. Instead, most of the curriculum seems geared toward turning out graduates who will step into executive marketing and public relations positions and conduct multimillion-dollar ad campaigns for major corporations.

Few business graduates seem to realize that selling products and services involves a lot of person-to-person contact. It means getting your hands dirty in day-to-day trench warfare with your competitor down the street. When was the last time you heard of a class on closing techniques as part of the core curriculum of the business or marketing department of any major college or university? Sales greats like Zig Ziglar, Jim Rohn, and Tom Hopkins are having astounding success teaching business and marketing graduates what they should have learned in business school. On fertile ground abandoned by our educational institutions, a multimillion-dollar training industry has grown by teaching about real-world marketing and selling — in particular, referral marketing, the systematic cultivation of word-of-mouth business.

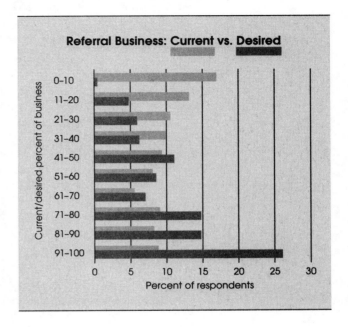

BRIDGING THE REFERRAL GAP

A SYSTEMATIC WAY to get referrals — that's what this book is about. In these pages you will learn a system that, although perhaps new to you, points the way back to an older, more satisfying way of doing business. It's a tried-and-true kind of commerce that has all but disappeared from our consciousness in the noise of national mass marketing.

The system we describe in this book will not only help you generate more referrals and make more money without spending a fortune on advertising or mass marketing, it will also reward you with satisfying personal and professional relationships in the process.

And if that's not enough to get your fires going, consider this:

YOU'LL NEVER, EVER HAVE TO MAKE ANOTHER COLD CALL.

A Natural Way to Do Business

Making the Commitment to Referral Marketing

ALMOST EVERY ENTERPRISE gets some of its business by referral. It's a natural phenomenon: if you provide good products or services, word gets around. Over the company phone or over a cup of coffee, one of your satisfied clients tells a friend or colleague good things about your business. It's also true, obviously, that if you've messed up royally, the friend or colleague gets an entirely different picture of your business — and you'll probably never know you've lost a potential customer.

Word of mouth is such a natural way of doing business that we usually don't give it a second thought. It's human nature to tell others about the good things we've discovered and caution them against making the same mistakes we've made. Whether you intend to or not, if you've satisfied some of your customers, you'll always get some business through referrals.

But here's the rub: if you want to get all of your business, or even *most* of your business, through referrals, you can't just sit back and wait for it to happen. You have to help it along.

Beyond Closing Sales: Opening Doors

BUILDING A SUCCESSFUL word-of-mouth business requires a systematic way of generating referrals. It calls for a commitment from you to devote a certain amount of time and effort to building relationships that will pay off in increased referrals. You have to learn a new way of doing business.

But, really, it's the way business used to be — when running a business meant serving a community of people you knew, trading with customers who were your friends and your friends' friends. The old ways are hard to find these days because we live in cities full of strangers. Typically, we work far from where we live, and far from where our friends and neighbors live.

So if you wish to run a successful business based on referrals, you can't just let the referral process take its own course. You need a new kind of business plan — a plan designed specifically to bring in referrals.

If you've been through business school, you've devoted a lot of learning time to getting the customer to commit to the purchase. You know that to close the sale, you have to overcome the buyer's skepticism. You have to achieve a certain level of trust — and sometimes building that trust is difficult. After all, you are a stranger.

What if you could start the process with a certain level of trust built in? What if you could get the buyer to seek you out because he has already begun to trust you, even before he's met you?

Getting business by referral begins with the understanding that there are people out there who want your services or products as badly as you want their business. The key to a successful referral-based business is putting the two of you together. It's not a random, passive process; it's a systematic, planned, active process that you can quantify and measure, as you will see in later chapters of this book.

Defining Our Terms

WHILE WE'RE AT IT, let's define some of the terms you will see in these pages. That will give you a glimpse of the sophisticated referral-generating system we are talking about.

Referral marketing, the goal of the process outlined in this book, is the practice of building a base of customers, clients, or patients by obtaining support from specific sources. A *Referral Marketing Campaign (RMC)* is a purposeful set of actions taken toward this end; your *Referral Marketing Plan* is the means you use to plan and implement your RMC.

Relationship development is the practice of establishing an acquaintanceship and cultivating from it a trusting friendship and a lasting professional association.

Your *Network*, with a capital *N*, is a systematically and strategically selected group of people on whom you can call as the need arises. It is a diverse, balanced, and powerful system of sources — people from all facets of the business world — that will provide the referrals, knowledge, and support you need in key areas of your business or profession.

In this book, you, the person who is seeking and expecting to get referrals, are the *vendor*. You'll be asking another person — your *source* — to provide you with a *referral*, that is, the name of a *prospect*, or prospective buyer of your product or service. Once the prospect decides to purchase a product or service from you or otherwise to provide you with a business opportunity, he becomes your *customer* or *client* (or, in some cases, *patient*).

Business opportunities are not limited to purchases by customers. A *business opportunity* is any situation that has the potential to generate revenue for your business. A friend might ask you to speak before a meeting of her service organization; although you are not paid, you meet several members who show an interest in hiring your services. Or perhaps a magazine editor asks you to write an article about your business specialty, thereby bringing your name to the attention of a much broader audience of potential customers.

Our Mission

WORD-OF-MOUTH MARKETING, getting new customers by referral from others, has been around since the first flint chipper began trading spear points for mammoth meat. What there has never been, however, is a truly systematic way of planning for, generating, and monitoring referral business.

Most traditional business plans include budgeting for advertising; few, however, take more than a bare-bones approach to measuring the costs and benefits of developing relationships and generating referrals — perhaps a line item for business lunches. That's the reason we wrote this book. We wanted to make referral marketing as tangible and as measurable as other promotional techniques, such as direct mail and newspaper advertising.

By including detailed financial planning and cost accounting for productive networking, you will create a truly comprehensive referral marketing plan for your business that that can be shared with and understood by investors, bankers, staff members, and business associates. It will contain vital information that you can use as an evaluation tool. It will let you identify and react more readily to current and potential problems; it will enable you to explain your successes and failures from a bottom-line perspective; it will keep you focused.

The Road Ahead

BUSINESS BY REFERRAL will lead you through a step-by-step planning process. At intervals you will be asked to turn to a "tool" (form or worksheet) in appendix A and fill in certain data. At certain points you will also be asked to summarize this information in appendix B, your Referral Marketing Plan (using as a guide the filled-in example shown in appendix C). Most of these tools are simple and easy to complete. But when you finish the process, you may be surprised at how much information you have recorded and how easy this will make it to implement your Referral Marketing Plan — the end result.

In the sidebar opposite this page is an outline of the plan you will create as you progress through the book, along with the chapters where it's discussed. And here's a little more detail about what's in the chapters:

Part II is about your business as it now stands, before you begin designing your Referral Marketing Campaign. Chapter 3 details how a business relationship evolves as an acquaintanceship matures through trust and mutual benefit into a profitable collaboration. Chapter 4 asks you to examine your business's mission, products, services, strengths, weaknesses, and competitive position. Chapter 5 lists fifteen ways your Network members can promote your business.

Part III is where you outline your Network. Chapter 6 describes the three main components of a Network; chapters 7, 8, and 9 show you how to build these components by listing the sources of support that are available to you; and chapter 10 helps you identify your Network's weak points and shore them up.

In part IV, you begin the process of making your connections.

Component	Chapter
1. Mission Statement	4
2. Products and Services	4
3. Target Market	4
4. Competition	4
5. Matching Needs and Prospective Sources	11
6. Tactics	12
7. Referral Marketing System	13, 14, 17
8. Time Budget	18
9. Calendar	18
10. Cost Budget	18
11. Sales and Referral Projections	19
12. Tracking and Evaluation	20

Chapter 11 outlines a simple, practical, thorough way to become better acquainted with your Network members, and chapter 12 lists eighteen ways to motivate them to help you achieve your goals and increase your referral business.

Part V kicks off the process of using your Network to implement your Referral Marketing Plan. Chapters 13 through 17 show you how to recruit your chosen referral sources, get them working effectively on your behalf, help them contact prospects for you, make your initial contacts with the prospects they send you, and share with your sources the results of these contacts and the benefits they bring you.

Part VI shows you in detail how to plan and monitor your Referral Marketing Campaign. Chapter 18 walks you through the process of budgeting your time and expenses and outlining your calendar; chapter 19 lets you forecast sales from referrals; and chapter 20 gives you a method of tracking, analyzing, and evaluating your results. Once you've completed the tools and activities described in this part (and available for photocopying in part VII, with filled-out examples of the Referral Marketing Plan), you'll have set up a systematic and predictable way to expand your business the most efficient way possible — through referrals.

YOUR COMMITMENT

NOTE WELL: we have said that each step in this process is easy. The key to making it all come together, however, is to take each and every step, from beginning to end. It won't happen overnight; it takes time to walk through the process. And once you have established your Network and started it working for you, it takes more time for the Network to grow, the referral-generating process to build up a head of steam, and the results to start coming in.

Doing business this new way requires a special ingredient that only you can supply: your commitment. You have to do more than just read and understand the book. You have to do more than just promise yourself you will get around to it. You have to commit to the process from the beginning. You have to take action.

THE PAYOFF

YOUR REWARD for developing a strong referral-based business can be high. Many businesses have become so adept at it that they get most of their sales through referrals and spend little or no money on advertising — and without cold calling. Some of these businesses hire most of their employees through referrals, manage complex financing arrangements, and even procure necessary products through referral contacts they have cultivated for many years.

You may even find the relationships you form with your referral sources more important than the dollars your new customers bring you.

But a referral-based business can reward you in ways beyond those measured in dollars. Dealing with people you like and trust is a better way to live and work than sparring with strangers all day long. You may even find the relationships you form with your referral sources more important than the dollars your new customers bring you. Such relationships are central to both the referral-generation process and the satisfaction you derive from your work.

Part

II

Laying the
Groundwork

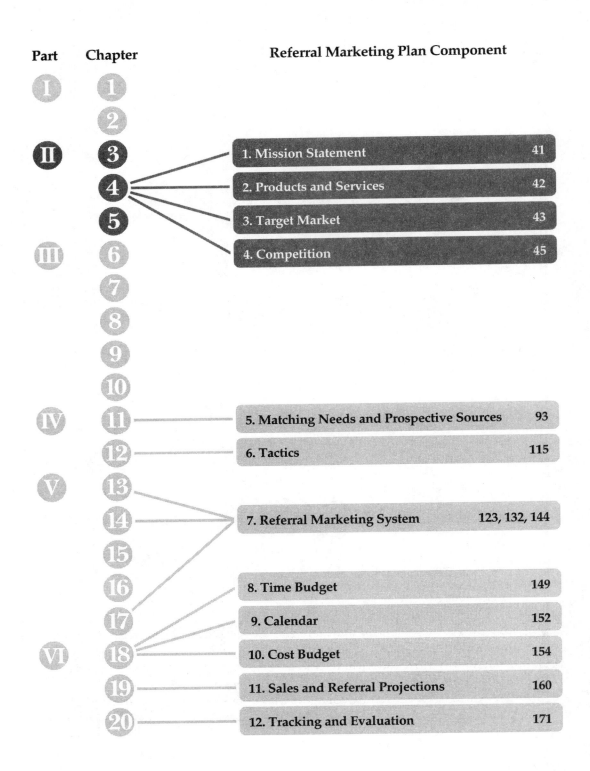

Part   Chapter   Referral Marketing Plan Component

3

It's All About Relationships

The Three Phases of Getting Acquainted

THE KEY CONCEPT in referral marketing is relationships. The system of information, support, and referrals that you assemble will be based on your relationships with other individuals and businesses. Referral marketing works because these relationships work both ways: they benefit both parties.

A referral marketing plan involves relationships of many different kinds. Among the most important are those with your referral sources, with prospects these referral sources bring you, and with customers you recruit from the prospects. These relationships don't just spring up full grown; they must be nurtured. As they grow, fed by mutual trust and shared benefits, they evolve through three phases: visibility, credibility, and profitability. We call this evolution the VCP model.

Any successful relationship, whether a personal or a business relationship, is unique to every pair of individuals, and it evolves over time. It starts out tentative, fragile, full of unfulfilled possibilities and expectations. It grows stronger with experience and familiarity. It matures into trust and commitment. The VCP model describes the process of creation, growth, and strengthening of business, professional, and personal relationships; it is useful for assessing the status of a relationship and where it fits in the process of getting referrals. It can be used to nurture the growth of an effective and rewarding relationship with a prospective friend, client, co-worker, vendor, colleague, or family member. When fully realized, such a relationship is mutually rewarding and thus self-perpetuating.

VISIBILITY

THE FIRST PHASE of growing a relationship is visibility: you and another individual become aware of each other. In business terms, a potential source of referrals or a potential customer becomes aware of the nature of your business — perhaps because of your public relations and advertising efforts, or perhaps through someone you both know. This person may observe you in the act of conducting business or relating with the people around you. The two of you begin to communicate and establish links — perhaps a question or two over the phone about product availability. You may become personally acquainted and work on a first-name basis, but you know little about each other. A combination of many such relationships forms a casual-contact network, a sort of de facto association based on one or more shared interests.

The visibility phase is important because it creates recognition and awareness. The greater your visibility, the more widely known you will be, the more information you will obtain about others, the more opportunities you will be exposed to, and the greater will be your chances of being accepted by other individuals or groups as someone to whom they can or should refer business. Visibility must be actively maintained and developed; without it, you cannot move on to the next level, credibility.

CREDIBILITY

REDIBILITY IS THE QUALITY of being reliable, worthy of confidence. Once you and your new acquaintance begin to form expectations of each other — and if the expectations are fulfilled — your relationship can enter the credibility stage. If each person is confident of gaining satisfaction from the relationship, then it will continue to strengthen.

Credibility grows when appointments are kept, promises are acted upon, facts are verified, services are rendered. The old saying that results speak louder than words is true. This is very important. Failure to live up to expectations — to keep both explicit and implicit promises — can kill a budding relationship before it breaks through the ground and can create visibility of a kind you don't want.

Credibility grows when appointments are kept, promises are acted upon, facts are verified, services are rendered.

To determine how credible you are, people often turn to third parties. They ask someone they know who has known you longer, perhaps done business with you. Will she vouch for you? Are you honest? Are your products and services effective? Are you someone who can be counted on in a crunch?

PROFITABILITY

HE MATURE RELATIONSHIP, whether business or personal, can be defined in terms of its "profitability." Is it mutually rewarding? Do both partners gain satisfaction from it? Does it maintain itself by providing benefits to both? If it doesn't profit both partners to keep it going, it probably will not endure.

The time it takes to pass through the phases of a developing relationship is highly variable. It's not always easy to determine when profitability has been achieved — a week? a month? one year? In a time of urgent need, you and a client may proceed from visibility to credibility overnight. The same is true of profitability; it may happen quickly, or it may take years — most likely, somewhere in between. It depends on the frequency and quality of the contacts, and especially on the desire of both parties to move the relationship forward.

Shortsightedness can impede full development of the relationship. Perhaps you're a customer who has done business with a certain vendor off and on for several months, but to save pennies you keep hunting around for the lowest price, ignoring the value this vendor provides in terms of service, hours, goodwill, and reliability. Are you really profiting from the relationship, or are you stunting its growth? Perhaps if you gave this vendor all your business, you could work out terms that would benefit both of you.

Profitability is not found by bargain hunting. It must be cultivated, and, like farming, it takes patience.

Profitability is not found by bargain hunting. It must be cultivated, and, like farming, it takes patience. Suppose you plant an apple tree in your front yard. You feed and water it, watch it grow from a sapling to a young tree. You wait for fruit to develop. After three years, no apples are visible, so you pull up the tree and move it to the backyard. The tree spends the next two years recovering from the move, and still it refuses to yield. So you move it again. As you can well imagine, this tree may never bear fruit for you — even if you don't manage to kill it.

Visibility and credibility are important in the relationship-building stages of the referral marketing process. But when you have established an effective referral-generation system, you will have entered the profitability stage of your relationships with many people — the people who send you referrals and the customers you recruit as a result.

Rediscovering Your Business

Finding Your Starting Point

F YOU HAVE little or no experience with referral marketing, it would be a mistake to jump into action without preparing yourself. Central to the referral-marketing process is getting people to send you referrals. To do so, they must know exactly what you do — what product or service you provide or make, how and under what conditions you provide it, how well you do it, and in what ways you are better at what you do than your competitors. You have to communicate this information to your sources. And to communicate effectively, *you* must know the same things.

It may seem a no-brainer; don't we all know what we do for a living? Yes, of course, most of us do. But can you communicate it clearly and simply to your potential sources? When you try to do so, you may find that you're not quite as clear on the facts as you thought. And if you can't tell your potential sources what you do or what you sell, how can they send you good referrals?

Before you map out where you're going to take your business with your Referral Marketing Campaign, pause and get a clear picture of where your business stands today. Try to answer, in simple terms, the following questions:

- Why are you in business?
- What do you sell?
- Who are your customers?
- How well do you compete?

Answering these questions for yourself will help you tell others what your business is about. This will make you more effective at implementing your comprehensive and systematic referral system.

KNOW YOUR MISSION

YOU MAY THINK you know why you're in business, but perhaps it's been years since you gave it serious thought. Now is a good time to reexamine why you're doing what you're doing. Ask yourself the following questions:

- What is my business mission? Beyond simply making a living, what are my long-range professional goals? Do I wish to become the standard by which my competitors are judged? Is it my dream to help make the world a better place?
- Where is my organization going? Am I achieving my mission? Am I making plans to accomplish it? How can I change policies, procedures, or personnel to improve my chances of achieving my mission?
- What environment is my organization operating in? What are the social, economic, and technological trends that affect the way I do business and my progress toward my goals?

● What are my core competencies? What do I like to do? What is it that I do better than my competitors? Is my business mission compatible with my values and aptitudes?

As business consultants, we've seen too many business professionals and companies try to be all things to all people. Starting out with the fundamentally sound goal of finding a niche that will make them successful, they go astray by changing direction every time a customer, advisor, or associate suggests a new product or service. The mission gets lost in a frantic scramble for business before the original idea ever gets a chance to pay off. We advise such companies to pause periodically to analyze their business and, if necessary, refocus on their mission and philosophy.

Ivan took his own advice when he founded Business Network Int'l. (BNI) in 1985. He determined that BNI's primary mission would be to pass business referrals to its members — specifically, "to help our members increase their business through a structured, positive, and professional word-of-mouth program." Since 1985, many people have brought BNI worthy ideas for new activities, programs, and projects that might help members in other ways. Although these are often very good ideas, many simply are not within BNI's focus. There are better companies, educational programs, and institutions than BNI, for example, to provide specialized sales and marketing training. BNI has rigorously avoided trying new ideas, even very worthwhile projects, that are not directly related to its mission or that would change its focus. This is, we feel, one of the reasons why, in a very short time, BNI has become the world's largest and most successful referral marketing organization.

● *MISSION STATEMENT: State your business mission as clearly and succinctly as you can. Then turn to appendix B and record it on component 1 of your Referral Marketing Plan. See example, appendix C.*

KNOW YOUR PRODUCTS AND SERVICES

W HEN YOUR REFERRAL MARKETING PLAN is working well, prospective customers buy from you the first time because they have been referred by your sources. They may continue to buy from you because they trust you and develop a good relationship with you. But whatever the reasons they come and whatever the reasons they stay, they are your customers primarily because they need your products or services.

A clear idea of your range of products or services is something your sources need to communicate to prospects. For each product or service you plan to market during your Referral Marketing Campaign, you must be able to articulate for your sources the answers to the following questions:

- What is the purpose of your product or service? What needs does it satisfy?
- How would you describe it? What are its shape, size, functions, key features, principal activities, benefits?
- How is your product or service delivered to the customer?
- How much does it cost, and under what conditions?

There are other questions concerning your products or services that you should answer for your own strategic purposes. Is your product becoming obsolete? Is there a newer or better way to provide the same service? What are the social and environmental effects of your product or service? Will economic or regulatory trends force you to change your products or services or the conditions under which you provide them? In the long term, will you be satisfied to continue to offer these products or services?

● **PRODUCTS AND SERVICES: List the products and services your business provides in component 2 of your Referral Marketing Plan (appendix B). See example, appendix C.**

Use the Product/Service Description Tool in appendix A-1 to describe each product or service that you offer in terms that will be clear to your sources and prospects. Then summarize your observations to complete the second component of your Referral Marketing Plan.

KNOW YOUR TARGET MARKET

WHAT IS YOUR TARGET MARKET? Most simply defined, it is the specific set of customers whose needs you are trying to meet. This is the audience, out of all those who might hear your message, for whom you design your marketing program. Instead of trying to sell your product or service to everyone in a market — everyone in your town, for example, or everyone who might see your television commercial — you should aim your message toward those who have the greatest potential need or desire for your product or service.

Even though you're pretty sure who your customers are, it's always good practice to step back now and then and examine your assumptions. You should be able to answer these questions for your sources:

- Who are your most likely customers?

- What do your customers come to you for?

- What is your real specialty, your area of expertise?

- What segment of your business gives you the most pleasure and the most profit?

Answering these questions will also give you a head start when you plan your referral strategy. Where should you concentrate your referral-gathering efforts? If you're a travel agent specializing in Caribbean cruises, your target audience is more likely to be found on the rosters of the American Association of Retired Persons than in Greenpeace. Should you publicize your services on talk shows? at trade shows? street fairs?

● *TARGET MARKET: In component 3 of your Referral Marketing Plan (appendix B), list the market or markets at which your business is aimed. See example, appendix C.*

It depends on the themes of those gatherings. Examine every event, every opportunity, to see whether your target audience is likely to be well represented. Then concentrate your marketing efforts where they will be most effective.

To get a clearer picture of your target market, you may find it helpful to complete the Target Market Description Tool in appendix A-2 and to identify the specific targets using appendix A-3. Summarize your results in the third component of your Referral Marketing Plan.

KNOW YOUR COMPETITIVE POSITION

O FIND OUT how you stack up against your competition, take a little time to analyze your competitive status. This exercise will help your understand and emphasize your unique selling position. How do you differ, and how can you position yourself for best competitive advantage?

43

There's no single formula for conducting a competitive analysis; it's mostly just good business sense. Try to stay aware of what your competition is doing and how your business stacks up against it. For example:

- Are your prices and costs competitive? Do customers who compare costs come back to you ?

- Do you compete effectively in terms of product or service quality?

- Are you seen as the vendor of choice? Why do people seek you out?

- Are you growing, losing ground, or just holding onto your market share? Are you waiting to see what will happen and hoping to react in time?

Staying competitive also implies being aware of trends and reacting to changes faster than your competitors. How will changes in technology and society affect the competition? Are your products or services more advanced than those of your competition? Do your competitors have the jump on you with online marketing? Understanding the driving forces in your industry — growth rates, shifts in buyer demographics, product and marketing innovations, the entry or exit of other competitors, changes in cost or efficiency, and so forth — will make you a top competitor.

● **COMPETITION: Turn to the Referral Marketing Plan (appendix B) and describe your competitive position in component 4. See example, appendix C.**

The Five Key Competitive Strategies

Your competitive strategy consists of the approaches and initiatives you take to attract customers, withstand competitive pressures, and strengthen your market position. According to Arthur Thompson and A. J. Strickland in *Strategic Management: Concepts and Cases*, there are five competitive strategies you should consider:

A low-cost leader strategy: striving to be the overall low-cost provider of a product or service that appeals to a broad range of customers. Notable examples are Sam's Club for general merchandise, Circuit City for consumer electronics, and Southwest Airlines for air travel.

A broad differentiation strategy: seeking to differentiate the company's product offerings from rivals' in ways that will appeal to a broad range of buyers. Nordstrom is known for its customer service policies and personnel; Whole Foods has established itself as a major food retailer with an emphasis on health foods and organic groceries.

A best-cost provider strategy: giving customers more value for the money by emphasizing both low cost and upscale difference, the goal being to keep costs and prices lower than those of other providers of comparable quality and features. The Saturn division of General Motors has managed to produce an economy car with customer satisfaction ratings that rival those of much more expensive cars.

A focused, or market-niche, strategy based on lower cost: concentrating on a narrow buyer segment and outcompeting rivals on the basis of lower cost. CompUSA and The Gap are examples of this strategy.

A focused, or market-niche, strategy based on differentiation: offering niche members a product

The number of business networking groups has grown dramatically in recent years. The fastest growing is BNI, which now has over 900 chapters in the United States and has established chapters in three other countries. BNI uses a market-niche strategy based on differentiation. It targets business owners and professionals who want to expand their referral business, and it limits each chapter's membership to one representative per specialty or profession. BNI's success also hinges largely on its training program. Directors receive a 250-page manual and are offered training twice a year in three-day conferences on strategies that give them a distinct competitive advantage in their markets.

or service customized to their tastes and requirements. Rolls-Royce sells a limited number of custom-built cars at the high end of the automobile prestige spectrum; men's big and tall shops specialize in selling mainstream styles to a limited market with specific physical requirements.

THE NEXT STEP

B Y NOW, you should have a pretty clear idea of how to tell others your business mission, the nature of your products and services, the people who constitute your target market, and the way you stack up against the competition. The ability to communicate this information to your sources and prospects will be invaluable as you begin to build your Network and formulate your plan to gain more and more business the most effective way — through referrals.

Fifteen Ways Others Can Promote You

How Your Network Can Boost Your Business

HAS ANYONE EVER said to you, "If there's anything I can do to help you with your business, let me know"? Did you respond, "Thank you. Now that you mention it, there are a few things I need"? Or did you say, "Well, thanks, I'll let you know"?

If you're like most of us, you aren't prepared to accept help at the moment it's offered. You let opportunity slip by because you haven't given enough thought to the kinds of help you need. You haven't made the connection between specific items or services you need and the people who can supply them. But when help is offered, it's to your advantage to be prepared and to respond by stating a specific need.

In the following chapters, you will begin to structure your Network to fit your business and professional needs, and you'll identify businesses and individuals who can provide specific kinds of help that you anticipate needing when problems arise or when you need to increase your visibility, credibility, or profitability. It's a good idea, then, to have in mind the kinds of help you will want your sources to provide.

How Your Network Members Can Help You

SYSTEMATIC REFERRAL MARKETING requires that you determine, as precisely as possible, the types of help you want and need. There are many ways your sources can help you promote yourself and your business and generate leads and referrals; we've chosen to discuss fifteen of them. Some are simple, cheap, and quick; others are complex, costly, and time-consuming.

1. Display Your Literature and Products

Your sources can exhibit your marketing materials and products in their offices or homes. If these items are displayed well, such as on a counter or a bulletin board, visitors will ask questions about them or read the information. Some may take your promotional materials and display them in other places, increasing your visibility.

2. Distribute Information

Your sources can help you distribute your marketing information and materials. For example, they can include a flyer in their mailings or hand out flyers at meetings they attend. A dry cleaner attaches a coupon from the hair salon next door to each plastic bag he uses to cover his customers' clothing; a grocery store includes other businesses' marketing literature in or on its grocery bags or on the back of the printed receipt.

3. Make an Announcement

When attending meetings or speaking to groups, your sources can increase your visibility by announcing an event you are involved in or a sale your business is conducting, or by setting up exhibits of your products or services. They can also invite you to make an announcement yourself.

4. Invite You to Attend Events

Workshops and seminars are opportunities to increase your skills, knowledge, visibility, and contacts. Members of personal or business groups that you don't belong to can invite you to their events and programs. This gives you an opportunity to meet prospective sources and clients.

5. Endorse Your Products and Services

By telling others what they've gained from using your products or services or by endorsing you in presentations or informal conversations, your Network sources can encourage others to use your products or services. If they sing your praises on audio- or videotape, so much the better.

6. Nominate You for Recognition and Awards

Business professionals and community members often are recognized for outstanding service to their profession or community. If you've donated time or materials to a worthy cause, your sources can nominate you for service awards. You increase your visibility both by serving and by receiving the award in a public expression of thanks. Your sources can pass the word of your recognition by word of mouth or in writing. They can even create an award, such as Vendor of the Month, to honor your achievement.

7. Provide You with Leads

A source can help you by passing along information she hears about someone who needs the kind of product or service you provide. Following through on such leads — for example, a rumor about a new company moving into the area or a news item about the troubles another business is having — could result in new business.

8. Provide You with Referrals

The kind of support you'd most like to get from your sources is, of course, referrals — names and contact information for specific individuals who need your products and services. Sources can also help by giving prospects your name and number. As the number of referrals you receive increases, so does your potential for increasing the percentage of your business generated through referrals.

9. Make Initial Contact with Prospects and Sources

Rather than just giving you the telephone number and address of an important prospect, a Network member can phone or meet the prospect first and tell him about you. When you make contact with the prospect, he will be expecting to hear from you and will know something about you.

10. Introduce You to Prospects

Your source can help you build new relationships faster by introducing you in person. She can provide you with key information about the prospect. She can also tell the prospect a few things about you, your business, how the two of you met, some of the things you and the prospect have in common, and the value of your products and services.

11. Arrange a Meeting on Your Behalf

When one of your sources tells you about a person you should meet, someone you consider a key contact, she can help you immensely by coordinating a meeting. Ideally, she will not only call the contact and set a specific date, time, and location for the meeting, but she will also attend the meeting with you.

12. Follow Up with Referrals They Have Given You

Your sources can contact prospects they referred to you to see how things went after your first meeting, answer their questions or concerns, and reassure them that you can be trusted. They can also give you valuable feedback about yourself and your products or services, information that you might not have been able to get on your own.

13. Publish Information for You

Network members may be able to get information about you and your business printed in publications they subscribe to and in which they have some input or influence. For example, a source who belongs to an association that publishes a newsletter might help you get an article published or persuade the editor to run a story about you.

14. Serve as a Sponsor

Some of your sources may be willing to fund or sponsor a program or event you are hosting. They might let you use a meeting room, lend you equipment, authorize you to use their organization's name, or donate money or other resources.

15. Sell Your Products and Services

Of all the kinds of support that a source can offer, the one that has the greatest immediate impact on your bottom line is selling your product or service for you. Your Network member could persuade a prospect to write a check for your product, then have you mail or deliver the product to your new customer. If you do so swiftly and cordially, you may gain a new lifelong customer.

Suppose a customer you know well tells you a friend of his wants to buy your product. How should you respond? By telling him to have his friend contact you? By asking for information about the friend? The correct answer is neither. While the interest is still hot, let your friend, the customer, take your product and sell it to his friend, the prospect (if he plans to see his friend in the near future, of course).

Marketing guru Jay Abraham has perfected the art of getting referrals from his colleagues — and a higher-powered group of colleagues would be hard to find. Vic Conant, president of Nightingale-Conant, sent a "Dear Friend" letter to his mailing list introducing Jay and telling how he had dramatically changed his business and his life. He enclosed materials describing Jay's seminars and encouraged the reader to attend one. Anthony Robbins sent a similar letter with information about Jay's book, and Denis Waitley's mailout offered Jay's audiotapes.

OTHER KINDS OF HELP

THERE ARE OTHER WAYS — with information, research, suppliers, and staffing, to name a few — your Network members can help you achieve business success. Keep a list of your needs with you at all times. Add to your list as other needs occur to you. Knowing how to match your needs with the right sources is key to obtaining the types of help you need — as you will see in chapter 11.

With a clear understanding of what you need and a handy reference in your briefcase or pocket, you'll be amazed how much easier it is to spot opportunities and find sources of support. You'll be better prepared to respond when someone says, "Let me know if there's anything I can do for you."

But remember — it's a two-way street. The fifteen support activities listed in this chapter are also things you can do to help your sources promote their businesses and generate referrals. So it's a good idea to keep a list of your Network members' needs with you as well. Helping your sources achieve their goals goes a long way toward building effective and rewarding relationships.

Designing
Your
Network

Part	Chapter	Referral Marketing Plan Component	
I	1		
	2		
II	3	1. Mission Statement	41
	4	2. Products and Services	42
	5	3. Target Market	43
III	6	4. Competition	45
	7		
	8		
	9		
	10		
IV	11	5. Matching Needs and Prospective Sources	93
	12	6. Tactics	115
V	13		
	14	7. Referral Marketing System	123, 132, 144
	15		
	16		
	17	8. Time Budget	149
		9. Calendar	152
VI	18	10. Cost Budget	154
	19	11. Sales and Referral Projections	160
	20	12. Tracking and Evaluation	171

Chapter 6

The Architecture of Your Network

Your Three-Part Support System

LET'S ASSUME YOU'VE DONE ALL THE THINGS we've recommended so far — defined your business, described your target market, identified your competition, and so forth. Let's assume also that you've identified several of the kinds of help listed in chapter 5 that you would like to receive. Now you're ready for the next step — constructing a referral-development system that will put you on the path to increasing your word-of-mouth business.

The first step is to establish what we have referred to as your Network.

WHAT'S A NETWORK FOR?

A S A SMALL-BUSINESS PROFESSIONAL or entrepreneur, how do you get advice and help when problems arise? How do you gather the information you need for making important business decisions? How do you identify your markets and locate potential clients? If you're like most people, you get help in times of need from individuals or businesses you don't know well. Instead of anticipating and planning for needs and emergencies, you are forced to react to every situation. You search the Yellow Pages or ask friends and associates to help solve problems or recommend solutions, even though these people may not have the necessary expertise and the sources they recommend may have little relevance to or experience with your business operation.

How do the big guys do it? A large organization usually has a formal structure, a management team that meets regularly to oversee and approve key activities and changes before other members of the organization implement them. Its purpose is to ensure that sound decisions are made, to facilitate communication and teamwork, and to protect assets. A typical management team might include the heads of the legal, marketing, personnel, operations, security, and finance departments. These individuals have ready access to vital resources — information, personnel, funding — and can plan ahead, see problems coming before they get big, and make informed decisions quickly in an emergency.

As a small-business owner or entrepreneur, of course, you don't have the built-in resources to form your own management team. What you need is the functional equivalent of a management team. Your Network is a systematically and strategically selected group of people on whom you can call as the need arises. It is a diverse, balanced, and powerful system of sources — people from all facets of the business world — that will provide referrals, information, and support in key areas of your business or profession, over both the short and the long term.

THE SYSTEMATIC APPROACH

E STABLISHING YOUR NETWORK begins with setting up a structure for your sources, much the same way a large company develops an organizational chart. We've developed a systematic, strategic approach to building this structure, an approach that has three essential function-based components:

- an Information Network
- a Support Network
- a Referral Network

We strongly recommend using this functional-component approach as you structure your Network and select its members. There are five advantages in doing this.

Advantage 1: A More Manageable Approach

The functional-component approach focuses your networking efforts, giving them a beginning and an end, or goal. Its specific guidelines and definitions show you how to identify prospective Network members. Other approaches to identifying and classifying your Network are more general, broad, and vague. Some, for example, classify sources as primary or secondary, contacts as strong or casual. Although the relative value of these sources may vary widely, you can't determine their value from the grouping alone. One may be more valuable in one circumstance, others more useful in a different situation.

Advantage 2: A Diversified, Balanced Support Team

The three components of your Network represent three kinds of assistance; each component has eight categories. By breaking down your Network into at least twenty-four categories of sources, you anticipate many different needs and reduce your chances of getting into a situation in which you don't know where to turn for help. Moreover, the strengths and weaknesses of your Network members balance each other.

Advantage 3: Overlooked but Cost-Effective Sources

Not only does this approach make you focus on selecting the best sources for each category, it also leads you to consider sources you might otherwise not have thought of. Defining in advance the kinds of help you will need lets you concentrate on searching your memory for people who fit each category. You may not think of some people immediately, but eventually, if you know someone who fits, you will remember him or her. If not, you will know what kind of person you should look for.

Advantage 4: A Way to Assess Strengths and Weaknesses

Our tools make it easy for you to identify the strengths and weaknesses of your sources. There are twenty-four slots to be filled (if you haven't customized your Network), and your goal is to identify at least one person in each category. An abundance of people in any category represents a strength; a void or shortage highlights a weakness.

Advantage 5: Ease of Finding, Remembering, and Accessing Your Sources

For most of us, it's easier to remember something if we've written it down. The three-part, functional-component approach requires you to list your sources; once you've done so, you'll remember their names more easily, and if you update the list regularly, as you should, they will become even more familiar.

How Do You Build a Network?

YOUR NETWORK IS NOT something you can start putting together when the need arises. When you need it, you need it now. You should begin developing relationships now with the people whose help you will need in the future. If you tell people they've been chosen to be on your "board of directors," and they've accepted the assignment, stay in touch with them. Do whatever you can to contribute to their success; you will find access to them becomes easier if you do.

The next four chapters will help you begin forming your Information, Support, and Referral Networks. They will show you how to identify the kinds of people you should include, then how to select the people you would like to have in these Network components, and how to strengthen them by shoring up their weak points. For each component, you'll need to take the following steps.

Step 1: Categorize Your Network Members

In each of the three components of your Network, we will identify eight general categories of people who are most likely to provide specific kinds of help — twenty-four categories in all. You should not feel confined to these categories; we use them partly to stimulate your thinking.

As you read the category descriptions and as names begin to occur to you, you will probably think of other people, and other categories of people, unique to your profession or your experience. Don't hesitate to include them in your Network if they can provide any kind of help you might need in building your referral business.

Step 2: Identify Your Network Members

Once you become acquainted with the three basic components of your Network and the eight categories of people in each component, your next step is to identify the people who will constitute your Network. To do so, you will find it helpful to fill out the appropriate Network Component Tool in appendices A-4, A-5, and A-6. Use at least one for each component of your Network.

On each sheet, first write the names of people you know, or know of, who fit in each category. Write down as many names as you can think of before you do anything else; try to name at least three people in each category, using names more than once only if necessary. Then go back and fill in the contact information for each name.

Pick the most qualified people — those who have the most experience, expertise, or contacts — in each category. These may be people with whom you have a close relationship or people you have never met, but the closer the better. If you can't think of anyone who fits, leave the category blank. One of your goals is to find the weaknesses in your Network — categories in which there's a void. These show you where you should concentrate your efforts when you seek new contacts.

Remember that those you list are only prospective members of your Network. As you become familiar with other elements of our referral-generating system and begin to apply its steps, you may discover that some of the people you've listed are not as appropriate as you thought. The same thing may also happen as you get to know these individuals better; you may find some less suitable than you thought, and others may not agree to participate. This is why you need at least three names per category — to have some assurance of ending up with at least one.

Write down as many names as you can think of. In some categories you may know 20, 50, or 100 people who fit. Ultimately, as you will see later, the size of your Network should be limited only by the number of people you can manage to maintain relationships with.

Your Information Network

*Sources
of Expertise
and Experience*

AS A BUSINESS PROFESSIONAL, you need a constant supply of information to achieve success. You must stay aware of trends and issues and keep up with rapid economic and technological changes to become and stay competitive. The Information component of your Network consists of your most knowledgeable sources, the people who can provide you with the knowledge and expertise you need to run a successful operation.

You may have discovered already that it is next to impossible to keep up with all this information on your own. There is simply too much of it, and your own inclinations and time limitations steer you toward some kinds of knowledge and cause you to neglect others. You may be strong in marketing and business planning but weak in personnel and legal matters.

Fortunately, the knowledge you lack is always someone else's specialty, so you can turn to others for help. This is what you are preparing to do when you set up your Network's Information component — a web of contacts who know and understand what you must do to achieve success in your profession or business, who have the experience to help you achieve your goals.

STEP 1: CATEGORIZE YOUR INFORMATION NETWORK MEMBERS

THERE ARE USUALLY AT LEAST a few people who can help you deal with certain issues or special problems that you may encounter in the business or profession you are in or are interested in entering. In lieu of specific knowledge, you must know in advance whom to contact and where to go to get the information you need. What sorts of people should you include in your Information Network?

1. People Like You

There are some real advantages to seeking out people who have the same interests and goals as you and who are trying to achieve the same thing you want to achieve. They are collecting the type of information you need, and vice versa; partnering with them can help you both get it faster by dividing the research effort.

2. People Who Are in Your Profession

As a rule, your best information sources will be people who are doing successfully what you want to do (perhaps in a different location or serving a different clientele). They will be aware of current trends and issues in your field and may have already faced some of the challenges you are now facing. Try to identify and speak with three to five individuals who fit this category. They will have current directories, manuals, and information about upcoming events related to your profession, as well as relationships with vendors you may need to hire.

3. People Who Were in Your Profession

Find out why these people are no longer in the profession. What happened to their business? What are they doing now? Did they make the right decision to leave the profession? Talk with people who were successful and people who were not. Depending on the industry and the length of time the person has been away from it, this information may be valuable in helping you plan.

4. Authors

People who write or produce books, articles, audiotapes, and videotapes on your profession are key subject experts. They usually have broad or deep knowledge about procedures, systems, technologies, tactics, and developments in your field. A few tips from these individuals could save you money and time.

5. Regulators

People who regulate, audit, or monitor professionals in your field can certainly tell you stories about the legal, procedural, and operational pitfalls that you might run into, and probably how to survive them. You may even discover legal loopholes that can make life and business easier.

6. Trainers

The wonderful thing about trainers is that they specialize in imparting knowledge. They help people understand the basics; they introduce new technologies, procedures, and techniques. Try to gain access to their training materials; if necessary, sign up for training sessions.

7. Consultants

Professionals use advisors and consultants to help them solve problems that they find difficult to handle alone or to deal with impending change. Some consultants are generalists, others, specialists. Most are skilled in assessing problems.

8. Members of Professional Organizations

People who are active members of trade, business, and professional organizations are prolific sources of information. Their membership gives them access to directories, newsletters, seminars, presentations, calendars of events, and more. By networking, they stay in touch with industry issues and trends. Spending time with them will help you discover new ways to do things.

STEP 2: IDENTIFY YOUR INFORMATION NETWORK MEMBERS

USING THE INFORMATION NETWORK COMPONENT TOOL (appendix A-4), first write the names of people you know, or know of, who fit each category. Write as many names as you can think of before you do anything else; try to name at least three people in each category. If necessary, you can use a name in more than one category, but it's better to come up with as many individuals as possible. Remember, it's information you're after, and more people means more information. Once you've written down as many names as you can think of, go back and fill in the contact information for each one.

Chapter 8

Your Support Network

Sources of Help and Encouragement

LEARN TO RELY ON THE PEOPLE who respect, admire, and love you; theirs are the purest motives for helping you. They are genuinely interested in you, mostly accept you as you are, and will usually do whatever they can to help you achieve any goal. They may not have the knowledge or information you need or the ability to bring you new clients, but if you direct their willing efforts, they can give you emotional, spiritual, physical, or financial support.

The gift of time can be a valuable resource. Members of your Network's Support component can help you at crucial times in your business. They can perform essential tasks, lend you money, encourage you, work for you, help you deal with an emergency, serve as a sounding board for your ideas, even fill in for you for a couple of hours. To make the most of this resource, learn about the talents, knowledge, and contacts these friends and supporters have to offer.

Step 1: Categorize Your Support Network Members

 HE PEOPLE MOST LIKELY to give freely of their support fall into eight categories:

1. Your Mentors

People who are or have been your mentors genuinely believe in you, care about you and your success, and can be counted on for honest feedback and encouragement. Perhaps even more than family members, they have insight into your abilities and know how to keep you focused. They may also help you in ways you aren't aware of by providing behind-the-scenes support and sponsorship.

2. People You Have Taught or Mentored

If you've been instrumental in another person's success by helping him gain professional knowledge and skills, that person probably owes you a debt of gratitude. These people are usually excited to hear from you and will remind you of how much they appreciate your support. They also open doors to business opportunities by constantly spreading positive word of mouth about you. Do the people you've mentored a favor: offer them the opportunity to pay you back. Most would be happy to support your efforts to achieve success.

3. People You Have Helped

People remember people who have done something for them. Can you identify people to whom you have donated money, time, or other gifts? Most will go out of their way to support you.

4. Your Co-Workers, Colleagues, Associates, and Classmates

Friends you have made in the course of your schooling and career are often friends for life. You are part of each other's history. You know, like, and respect each other. Of course, you may be reluctant to call upon a friend for help because you don't want to admit you need it. But don't let your ego get in the way; use these sources. A true friend will be eager to help and will not think any less of you, nor make you feel diminished, for asking.

5. Your Family and Close Friends

You may take your family and personal friends for granted, but they are perhaps your most reliable source of support. Don't ignore them. Keep in mind, however, that some may be more reliable than others.

6. Other Members of Nonbusiness Groups

People you have worked with outside of business — members of neighborhood watch groups, apartment associations, community youth programs — may be willing to support you in activities outside the group's normal scope. Members of community service organizations such as Kiwanis and Lions Clubs usually make it a point to contribute to the success of other members. Join, participate, donate generously of your time, and let others help you in your endeavors.

7. Your Former Managers, Supervisors, and Instructors

Your former managers, supervisors, and instructors — those you admired, at least — are often familiar with your work habits, ethics, values, character, abilities, and interests. They know what it takes to get you to perform at your highest level. Often, like surrogate parents, they feel responsible for your success. Should you take advantage of this parental instinct? Of course!

8. Your Church Leaders, Members, and Groups

When it comes to giving, few places can match the spiritual and emotional support that churches provide in abundance. If you belong to a religious organization, you are bonded to others through a shared faith.

It would be a mistake not to seek the backing of your church leaders and other members. If on occasion you need them, don't hesitate to use the church's support services and groups.

STEP 2: IDENTIFY YOUR SUPPORT NETWORK MEMBERS

TURN TO THE SUPPORT NETWORK COMPONENT TOOL (appendix A-5) and write the names of all the people you know who fit into each category — as many names as you can. Use names more than once only if you have to. The more names, the better; if one person is unable to provide the kind of support you need at a particular moment, you'll have others to fall back on. Finally, fill in the contact information for each name.

Chapter 9

Your Referral Network

Sources of Business Opportunities

IF YOU CAN RUN A BUSINESS entirely on the sales you make through referrals, you'll be the envy of all business owners. Someone — customer, colleague, associate, friend — tells someone else about you or tells you about a prospect, and the end result is a sale. Referrals are your most profitable Network component, and the only way to get them is through other people.

Not all referrals result in business. The likelihood of a sale depends on the method used by the referral source to contact the prospect, the quality of their business relationship, and other factors. Some are more likely to encounter good prospects than others; some will be more motivated to give you referrals. Savvy professionals who know and cultivate their most likely referral sources get the largest number of high-quality referrals, and the more referrals they get, the more revenue they generate in the long run.

STEP 1: CATEGORIZE YOUR REFERRAL NETWORK MEMBERS

OME OF YOUR BEST SOURCES for referrals will, of course, be the same people you consider primary sources of support and information. Others will come from entirely new categories of people, some of which may surprise you. Your best prospective referral sources fall into eight categories.

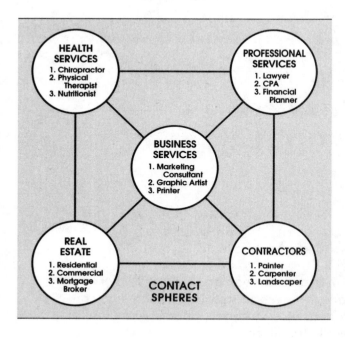

1. People in Your Contact Sphere

A contact sphere — a group of businesses or professions that complement, rather than compete with, your business — can be a steady source of leads. It's almost a sure thing: if you put a caterer, a florist, an entertainer, a printer, a meeting planner, and a photographer in the same room for an hour, you couldn't stop them from doing business. Each has clients who can benefit from the services of the others. This is why a wedding often turns out to be, on the side, a business networking and referral-gathering activity.

2. Satisfied Clients

One of your best referral sources is satisfied clients. Having firsthand experience with your products or services, they are true believers and can communicate convincing testimonials. Keep track of these clients; they are your fans, your best promoters, and they can be very effective in helping others decide to do business with you. Of course, a dissatisfied client is equally effective in turning prospects away from you.

3. People Whose Business Benefits from Yours

Of the eight kinds of people in your Referral Network, none stand to gain more than those who get more business when you get more business: business suppliers and vendors, for example. If you sell workbooks, the printer who prints them for you benefits. A related business located close to you may benefit from your customers — for example, a health-food restaurant located next to your family fitness center. In these circumstances, it is obviously in the other businesses' self-interest to give you referrals.

Robert conducted a workshop on networking for the Orange County Water Association, a professional group composed primarily of engineers. Neil, one of the participants, liked the workshop so much that he ended up, on his own initiative, writing to the Los Angeles chapter of the association to recommend that Robert do a workshop for them. Neil's letter cited specific benefits he got from the workshop and how it would help the Los Angeles chapter. The president of the association responded with interest. Neil called Robert and volunteered to coordinate the arrangements.

Only someone who believes in you would go to such lengths to promote your business. It is people like Neil, who believe in your products or services, who can do the most in recommending referrals. Neil, a member of the association, could articulate the reasons other engineers needed the workshop, and he knew the specific benefits they would derive from it even better than Robert did.

4. Others with Whom You Do Business

Perhaps your business doesn't have anything to do with dentistry or hairstyling or automobiles, but every day you do business with dentists, hairstylists, and auto mechanics. By contributing to the success of their business, you gain their goodwill; to keep you as a customer, they're inclined to help you secure customers of your own. If you've been using their services for some time, these vendors probably know what you do and that you're a reliable, trustworthy person. Sometimes this is all the recommendation a potential client needs.

5. Staff Members

Except for customers, no one understands better than staff members how your products or services perform. Not just sales and marketing staff — generating sales is what they were hired to do — but part-time or full-time staff members in administration, production, and other functions give your business a boost when they talk with friends, neighbors, associates, and people they meet in their daily lives. Keep them happy; a disgruntled employee can do your business a lot of harm.

Don't overlook former staff members, either. Working for your company will always be part of their history, and often part of their conversation with prospects as well.

6. People to Whom You've Given Referrals

You're more likely to get a referral from someone to whom you've given a referral. The more you give, the more you'll get.

7. Anyone Who Has Given You Referrals

People who give you referrals for business or direct others to you for networking or advice are demonstrating that they think highly of you and what you do. If they didn't, they would refer people elsewhere. Strengthen and nurture these prospective referral sources; don't take them for granted. Show your appreciation with personal gestures and by referring prospects to them. Call on them for further referrals, but don't abuse their generosity. Maintain the business standards that earned you their respect.

8. Other Members of Business Referral Groups

Referral groups are set up by their members mainly to exchange leads and referrals. A typical weekly meeting of such a group includes time devoted exclusively to networking and referring business. If you're a member, this is what you signed up for: ready access to potential new clients. To encourage communication and limit possible competitive conflicts, business referral groups often restrict membership to one person per profession or specialty.

STEP 2: IDENTIFY YOUR REFERRAL NETWORK MEMBERS

USING THE REFERRAL NETWORK COMPONENT TOOL (appendix A-6), write as many names as you can of people you know, or know of, who fit into each category. You can use a name more than once if necessary, but try to name at least three people in each category. After all, these are your primary sources for referrals, and getting more referrals is the reason you're reading this book. Once you've written down all the potential referral sources you can think of, fill in the information on how to contact each one.

Chapter 10

Making Your Network Stronger

Three Ideas for Intensifying Your Network

I T HAS PROBABLY OCCURRED TO YOU that, if certain kinds of needs arose in your business, you would have no idea where to turn for information, advice, or assistance. This is not unusual. Often we overlook or ignore a potential need until it becomes a pressing need. This is human nature; you're usually too busy just taking care of day-to-day business to think about emergencies that might or might not occur.

But we all know — even those of us who were never into scouting — that it's best to be prepared. Indeed, that's largely what this book is about. Being prepared for a wide variety of situations not only serves as insurance but also helps you establish and maintain the contacts you need to expand your referral-based business. Even if an emergency never happens, the work you do in preparing for one is not wasted; it goes into building your Network.

Your Network is only as strong as its weakest link. The final step in constructing it is to make it bigger, stronger, and more valuable — to intensify it. Here are three ideas that can help you do this.

IDEA #1: CUSTOMIZE YOUR NETWORK

DON'T CONFINE YOURSELF to the Network components and categories we've presented here; create others appropriate for your business or profession. For example, you might create an "industry" component with several categories of its own — engineers with whom you've collaborated, patent attorneys you know, and so on. Or you might add new categories to one or more of the existing components. Handle your new components and categories just like the others: identify at least three individuals per category.

IDEA #2: BUILD YOUR NETWORK

REMEMBER ONE OF THE KEY REASONS you're setting up your Network: to create your own de facto management team, a ready group of experts and contacts who can give you advice on planning and growing your business and help you handle any problems that arise. After all, if you need legal advice, would you rather know ahead of time whom to call, or just thumb through the Yellow Pages or newspaper ads? How about other areas of business — printer, secretary, interior decorator, security guard, banker, travel agent, collection agent, personnel agent? Do you know someone in each of these businesses with the experience and expertise you seek?

According to Harvey Mackay's *Dig Your Well Before You're Thirsty*, you should develop sources before you need them. By identifying and acquainting yourself with individuals before you need their products, services, or information, you'll save time and money and make more intelligent business decisions. And you'll know the approximate value and cost of the products and services before you need them.

> One of the key reasons you're setting up your Network is to create your own de facto management team, a ready group of experts and contacts who can give you advice on planning and growing your business and help you handle any problems that arise.

The Universal Business Network Tool (appendix A-7) will help you discover areas where you can intensify your Network. The categories represent occupations that most business owners and professionals will need to know something about. Although meeting these types of people is not urgent, you should begin adding them to your list and periodically get in touch with them. Think of this list as your personal Yellow Pages.

IDEA #3: FILL IN THE VOIDS

NOW THAT YOU'VE IDENTIFIED members of your Information, Support, and Referral Network components and completed the Universal Business Network Tool, you should more easily be able to spot the voids and weaknesses in your Network. By seeking individuals who work in these areas and filling in the voids, you will enhance the diversity, size, and strength of your Network. Use the Business Network Voids Tool (appendix A-8) to summarize the voids you have identified.

THE END OF THE BEGINNING

BY NOW, you should be well on your way to forming a powerful and diversified team of sources for your business or professional practice, a Network that will provide you with information, support, and referrals. This systematic approach should be helping you structure your Network, identify prospective members, and spotlight areas where you need to concentrate your efforts.

Several questions now arise. Have you selected the right people? Have you overlooked people you should have listed or included people you should not have? The answers depend on how well you know the individuals you have selected and how well you know your business. Perhaps you've made assumptions or failed to recall key facts about them.

The next chapter will outline five things you need to know about your prospective Network members. Using these items as a guide to enhancing your acquaintance with them, you will then be able to determine whether you've made the right choices.

Finding and Cultivating Your Contacts

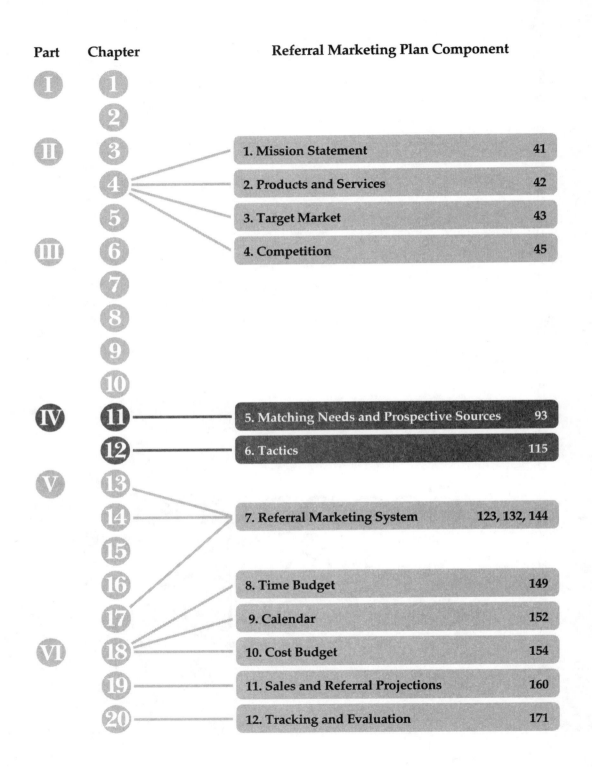

Part   Chapter   Referral Marketing Plan Component

11

Getting to Know Your Network Members

The GAINS Approach to Getting Acquainted

IN *SWIM WITH THE SHARKS WITHOUT BEING EATEN ALIVE*, Harvey Mackay says that for success in generating sales, you must know your customer: "Armed with the right knowledge, we can outsell, outmanage, outmotivate, and outnegotiate our competitors." We believe that for success in generating referrals, it's just as crucial to know your sources — the members of your Network.

By now, you should have made a list of a least some of the people you would like to include in your Network. Before you recruit them, though, you need to determine how appropriate your choices are. Are your information and assumptions about each prospective member's background and expertise correct? What's your relationship with each? How well are you acquainted? Do you know him well enough to trust him? Is your relationship with her profitable for either of you?

In this chapter we will present five things that you and the members of your Network should know about each other. We will also tell you how to get this information and use it to strengthen both new and established relationships by increasing your

- resourcefulness;
- access to valuable resources;
- ability to influence and inspire others;
- effectiveness in utilizing resources;
- ability to identify business opportunities for you and others you know;
- sphere of influence; and
- visibility, credibility, and profitability.

THE FIVE ELEMENTS OF THE GAINS EXCHANGE

IN OUR VIEW, there are five things you should get to know about anyone you wish to establish a relationship with — not just business contacts, but employers, employees, association leaders and members, potential life partners. These five things are not mysterious secrets; they are facts we are exposed to every day but often pay little attention to because we are not aware of the benefits we can accrue by sharing them. We call this sharing the GAINS Exchange:

- Goals
- Accomplishments
- Interests
- Networks
- Skills

If you know the GAINS categories and use them effectively, you can strengthen your relationships, create stronger organizations, and live a more rewarding, productive, and enjoyable life. This is also a two-way street; not only should you know these things about others, you should share with them the same information about yourself.

Goals

Goals are the financial, business, educational, and personal objectives you want or need to meet for yourself and for people who are important to you. They could be problems you want to resolve or decisions you need to make, either immediately or down the road; for example,

- lose twenty pounds,
- relocate to Chicago,
- find another job within the next six months,
- raise $1,000 for the homeless,
- follow up with twenty-five prospects per month, or
- write a 200-page book by the end of the year.

Whatever they are, you need to define your own goals clearly and specifically (as you did in chapter 4), and you need to have a clear picture of the other person's goals. Indeed, the best way to develop a relationship is by helping someone achieve something that's important to her. If you do, she'll remember you when you need help achieving your goals. You'll become valuable sources for each other, and your relationship will endure.

Once a month, Robert talks with Terry Mayfield, one of his speaking colleagues. They update each other about their progress and next month's business goals. This exchange has proven very valuable. It helps them discover how they can support each other more effectively. One month Robert told Terry he was going to learn everything he could about how to use talk radio to promote his new book. To Robert's surprise, Terry offered to let him borrow a four-cassette program, developed by Joe Sabah, entitled *How to Get on Talk Show Radio All Across America*. Robert had no idea that Terry had such a valuable resource.

You may have friends and associates who have information and resources that could help you achieve your goals, but to reap the benefits of these relationships, you have to share your goals with them. Know what you want and need. Use the GAINS Profile tool (appendix A-9) to list your goals. Return to it when listing your accomplishments, interests, networks, and skills, as outlined in the rest of this chapter.

Accomplishments

Some of your best insight into others comes from knowing what goals they have achieved, what projects they've completed, what they have accomplished both for themselves and for others. Accomplishments, whether as student, employee, organization member, parent, friend, sports fan, or neighbor, tell you more about a person than any number of intentions or attitudes. Your knowledge, skills, experiences, character, values, and beliefs can be surmised from your achievements. Recruiters assess job seekers' employment potential based on their accomplishments.

Your accomplishments don't have to be worthy of making the newspapers. Simple accomplishments that can tell a lot about the goals you set and how you achieve them include

- writing a magazine article,
- building a brick wall,
- reading *War and Peace,*
- preparing a French dinner,
- raising four kids,
- walking five miles, and
- creating a marketing plan.

People like to talk about the things they're proud of. Engage potential Network members in casual conversation; encourage them to talk about their accomplishments. You will gain insight into how appropriate they will be as Network members.

Be ready to share your accomplishments with people you know and people you meet. You will naturally downplay some of them because of

---

GAINS Profile

Use this form to record goals, accomplishments, interests, networks, and skills — your own, or those of your Network members or others with whom you want to build a relationship. Use one form per individual; attach sheets as necessary. Date each entry so you will know how old the information is. Use the other side of this form to record information that doesn't fit one of the categories listed.

Name *Ulysses S. Grant*   Date *4/4/62*

Goals   *Settle disagreement with Gen. Johnston's army in southern Tennessee; recruit Jeb Stuart to Union cause; run for president (wait until end of war)*

Accomplishments *Managed hardware business; overran Fort Henry; invaded Kentucky*

Interests   *Cigars, bourbon, military history*

Networks   *Association of Yankee Generals; Distilled Spirits of the Month Club*

Skills   *Supervising large groups of unskilled workers; creating and resolving conflicts; managing "just in time" logistics and inventories*

---

modesty or because you consider them insignificant or don't think you did as good a job as you should have. Remember, however, that others may think more highly of these accomplishments than you do.

As you develop your list of accomplishments on the GAINS Profile tool, include not only the ones you are particularly proud of but also any others that may do you credit.

Interests

Your interests — the things you enjoy doing, talking about, listening to, or collecting — can help you connect with others. People are more willing to spend time with those who share their interests or know something about them. Interests may include such pastimes as

- playing sports,
- reading books,
- collecting coffee mugs,
- watching *Jeopardy*,
- listening to country music, or
- traveling to foreign countries.

Sharing your accomplishments may lead to fortuitous surprises. During a break at a workshop he was attending, Robert mentioned to Ed Poll, a professional speaker and attorney of ten years, that he was scheduled to speak to the Southern California Deli Council, a perishable foods industry association. Ed replied that he was familiar with the council because he and his father owned a pickle business. He gave Robert valuable guidance on customizing his presentation. If Robert had not mentioned this accomplishment — being invited to speak to the Deli Council — he would not have learned of Ed's connection with the industry nor benefited from Ed's experience with the council.

Knowing other people's interests makes it easier to find gifts they will appreciate — including information of value to them. Let them know your interests as well; if you and your Network source share many of the same interests, it will strengthen your relationship.

Passions are your most important interests. A passion is something you love to do, something you could do all day long without encouragement or compliments from others. You can even be passionate about something without being good at it — but with passion, it's unlikely that you will fail to improve.

What are your interests? What are your passions? What do you love to do? Use the GAINS Profile tool to list your interests.

Networks

A network starts with any group (formal or informal), organization, institution, company, or individual you associate with for either business or personal reasons. You have many networks, both formal and informal. If you graduated from Stanford University, then one of your networks is Stanford. If you work for Wal-Mart and take your daughter to Girl Scout meetings, your networks include Wal-Mart and the Girl Scouts. If you survived the 1994 Northridge, California, earthquake, you are a de facto member of the Survivors of the Northridge Earthquake network.

As the saying goes, "It's not what you know but whom you know" — and to that you can add, "whom the people in your Network know." Each of us has sources in abundance that we never use. Each member of your Network is part of several other networks; each of your prospective sources is connected, directly and indirectly, with hundreds, even thousands, of people you don't know. If you can tap the resources represented by these unknown network members, you can

- significantly increase the potential for expanding your Network and your return from networking;
- assess the potential use and value of the help your networking members can provide;
- select your most profitable sources more effectively;
- direct and use your sources more effectively; and
- become a better source for your prospective sources.

To acquaint his audiences with his networks and interests, Robert distributes a profile listing current and past companies he has worked for, schools he has attended, and memberships in professional and community organizations (opposite). The response has been gratifying; people often come up to him with the news that they have worked for the same organization or attended the same school. Their common interest leads to further opportunities to get acquainted. Sharing your networks and interests will help you build relationships faster — relationships that lead to business opportunities.

Use the GAINS Profile tool to list a few of your networks.

A Profile of ROBERT DAVIS
(AKA: Dr. Follow-Up)

Business name: Robert Davis Associates

Business started: 1989

Passion: Professional speaking

Personal: Born in Los Angeles, California. Married in 1980 to Belinda, an elementary school teacher, and has one daughter, Adhana, born in 1987

Occupation: Professional speaker, trainer, author, and consultant for the insurance industry. Master subjects include generating referrals, developing professional relationships, overcoming the negative effects of perfectionism and career management. Vice president, Drake Beam Morin, Inc. (world's largest outplacement company)

Previous occupations:

Human Resources Manager	Restaurant Host
Substitute Teacher	Executive Recruiter
Cashier/Sales Representative	Night Auditor

Previous employers:

Federal Home Loan Bank of San Francisco	First Interstate Bank
Ontario-Montclair School District	The Broadway
Associated Bankers Search	Westin Hotels

Schools attended:

University of San Francisco (MA)	Pomona College (BA)
Compton Community College	Cal. State Univ., Los Angeles

Affiliations/memberships:

National Speakers Association	Black Women's Network
American Society for Training & Development	
Spanish Trails Business & Professional Development Institute	

Mentors and inspirational role models:

Magic Johnson, LA Lakers superstar

Willie Jolley, speaker and author, *It Only Takes a Minute to Change Your Life*

Dr. Ivan Misner, founder of BNI and author

Steve Stewart, author of eight books and several audiotapes

Alexis Woods, Graduate Career Services director, University of Oregon

Hobbies: Karaoke, bridge, chess, basketball, and travel

Skills

The more you know about the talents, abilities, and assets of the people in your Network, the better equipped you are to find competent, affordable service when you or someone you know needs help. And when you're trying to round up business opportunities or simply to become more visible, your chances are much better when others know about your skills in, for example,

- negotiating,
- interviewing,
- budgeting,
- driving,
- fund-raising,
- selling, or
- hiking.

Our experience in working with prospective business owners, entrepreneurs, business professionals, and job seekers has shown that a lot of people are unaware of all the skills they possess. If you're like most, you simply perform a service or do a job without giving much thought to the skills and knowledge you use. To help you inventory your skills reliably and completely, use the Skills Inventory (opposite), then list your skills on the GAINS Profile tool.

DISCOVERING OTHERS' GAINS

THERE ARE SEVERAL WAYS to gather information about the GAINS of your prospective Network members or anyone else you may deal with. All of them are simple; none require special skills.

Listen

The easiest way to find out about a prospective Network member is simply to engage him in ordinary conversation. If you listen carefully, you may learn about a problem he's trying to solve (a goal), the project he just completed (an accomplishment), the basketball game he watched yesterday (an interest), his attorney sister (a member of one of his networks), and the software he used to design an overhead (a skill).

Skills Inventory

The following are some of the skills you might need to perform in many different professions. Which of these skills have you used in your career? Which are your strongest skills, the ones you are most successful at and prefer to use? List these first on your Gains Profile; then list any others that you have.

Administering organizations	Maintaining records
Allocating funds	Making recommendations
Analyzing information	Managing organizations
Analyzing organizational needs	Marketing products or services
Analyzing problems	Mediating
Appraising values	Monitoring progress
Arranging social events	Motivating employees
Assembling equipment	Negotiating contracts
Auditing accounts	Operating equipment
Auditing operations	Organizing tasks
Brainstorming	Persuading
Calculating numerical data	Planning activities
Checking accuracy	Preparing publicity
Coaching	Preparing reports
Communicating	Presenting ideas
Compiling data	Programming computers
Conducting meetings	Promoting events
Coordinating computer networks	Protecting property
Coordinating tasks	Raising funds
Corresponding in writing	Recording information
Counseling	Recruiting
Creating work environments	Repairing equipment
Delegating responsibility	Researching
Designing information systems	Scheduling
Developing projects	Selling
Directing programs	Setting agendas
Disseminating information	Setting policy
Distributing products	Solving problems
Editing	Troubleshooting
Entertaining	Others: _____
Establishing standards	_____
Evaluating results	_____
Evaluating services	_____
Maintaining equipment	

It's not always that easy, of course, but once you discover an individual's interests or — even better — his passions, you tap into information that will help you build a much stronger relationship, particularly if you share that interest or passion. On an early-morning walk with his neighbor Richard, Robert discovered one of Richard's passions. They plodded silently for a while — it usually took Richard half the walk to wake up — then they began to talk. The subject of sailing came up. Richard became animated, energized, excited, telling Robert all about his experience and interest in sailboats. Now, whenever Robert wants to get Richard's attention, he simply talks about sailboats.

Observe

Want to know more about your prospective Network member? Be a detective. Watch where he goes and with whom he spends his time. What kind of car does he drive? What does his bumper sticker say? What books does he read? What colors does he wear? When you see him away from the office, is he carrying a tennis racket, a toddler, a backpack, a sack of fertilizer? Does he wear a T-shirt that says BUNGEE BANZAI? You'll be surprised at how much you can learn by just watching and thinking about what you see.

Ask Questions

Do you have a good, open, friendly relationship with your prospective Network member? If you do, your best way of finding out her GAINS may simply be to ask her. If that seems too direct, however, you can learn a lot by asking indirect, conversational questions. What exciting things did she do this weekend? What good movies has she seen lately? How has her year gone? This is the way most of us get to know our friends and acquaintances.

Review Written Materials

Another way to discover your Network prospect's GAINS is to review all of his promotional materials — brochures, business cards, newsletters, press releases, notes — that you can get your hands on. If he's made a record of his knowledge or skills, such as a book or an instructional audiotape or videotape, get a copy and pay close attention.

Ask Others

Anyone who has contact with a prospective Network member or other person you deal with is a source of information. Without coming across as an investigator, ask her a few questions about her relationship with your target. For example, how long has she known X? How well does she know X? What opportunity has she had to work with X?

Share Your GAINS

People are more likely to share information with you if you share information with them. Take the initiative: share a goal, accomplishment, or interest with a prospective Network member. He will probably respond in kind. Robert gets the ball rolling by describing some of his priorities. Then, looking for an opportunity to offer help, he asks, "What are some of your priorities for this week or month?"

When he asks this question, Robert never knows what sort of help he will end up providing. One of his friends was looking for a good female mentor; he gave her two recommendations. To another friend, struggling with handling a new job assignment, he offered a suggestion that led to the friend's getting more help. After reading in the magazine of an association he was scheduled to address that the group's president wanted to increase the number of members from the retail industry, he sent her twelve suggestions. She will probably remember him, and he expects to discuss his suggestions with her in more detail.

RECORDING THE GAINS YOU DISCOVER

As YOU DISCOVER THE GAINS of the people you are interested in, keep a record; otherwise, you're likely to forget important information. Use the GAINS Profile tool to record the facts you learn about your most important contacts. When you don't have a GAINS Profile with you, keep detailed notes on whatever you have (you could even call your home phone and leave yourself a message). Label each item G, A, I, N, or S for easy reference. Later, add the new information to that person's GAINS Profile, or simply drop the note into his file.

GAINS TOO EASY?

IF YOU THINK that getting to know the GAINS of the people you deal with is too easy and you need a greater challenge, we have two recommendations:

- First, take the quiz in appendix A-10 to test your knowledge of each member of your Network.

- If you feel the need for an even greater challenge, get a copy of Harvey Mackay's *Swim with the Sharks* and test your knowledge using his 66-question customer profile.

QUALITY TIME

HOW WELL DO YOU KNOW the people you want to include in your Network? Chances are you have a little homework to do. You can't know everything about them, though; that's why we recommend that you focus on five key items — their GAINS.

Art Radtke, executive director of BNI's D.C. and Virginia chapter, uses a handy metaphor (complete with visual aids) to illustrate why you and your referral sources should get better acquainted with each other. Pretend you're a kid with a whiffle bat; your source is throwing you whiffle balls to hit. Your bat represents what you know about your source; the ball is what your source knows about you. With a skinny bat and a tiny ball, you'll find yourself striking out a lot. But if your source throws you a big, fat whiffle ball and you swing at it with a great big bat, you're more likely to hit a home run. It's the overlap factor — the space where the bat and the ball overlap — that increases your batting average.

Spend more time with the people you already know, particularly with those you believe you know well. Concentrate on learning these five essentials — their goals, accomplishments, interests, networks, and skills. Be prepared to discover new things. Find overlapping areas of knowledge and interest. Make sure you give back the same kinds of information. The more they know about you, the faster your name will come to mind when an opportunity arises in which your products, services, knowledge, skills, or experience might play a part.

MATCHING NEEDS WITH SOURCES

NOW THAT YOU'VE IDENTIFIED the kinds of support you need (chapter 5) and gotten better acquainted with your Network members, you're ready to make a preliminary decision about which of your prospective sources can provide you with the help you want.

Based on what you know about your Network members, determine the type of help you prefer from each. At this point, consider primarily each Network member's qualifications to provide the specific kind of product or service you need. Other factors that will influence how you match needs and sources include the Network member's availability, flexibility, and interests. You may have sources that are capable, but if they're not interested in helping you or don't have time to help you, it's not a good match.

You may not yet have enough information to identify a source for every need, but now you know where to focus your research. The more you know about your prospective sources, the easier the matching process will be. You will discover, inevitably, that some of your sources do not have the talent you thought they had, and others will have capabilities you weren't aware of.

Matching Needs and Prospective Sources

Help Needed	Sources to Contact
Publicity	Al Sharpton
Insurance	Lloyd Wausau
Transportation	Craig Breedlove

● **MATCHING NEEDS AND PROSPECTIVE SOURCES:** *In component 5 of your Referral Marketing Plan (appendix B), match your needs with the prospective sources best positioned to help you fulfill them.*

Eighteen Ways to Motivate Your Sources

*Inspiring Your
Network Members
to Help You*

NOW THAT YOU'VE IDENTIFIED your strategic sources — the members of your Network — how do you go about generating information, support, and referrals from them? Some people use what might be called the "hope" strategy: they provide great products and service and then sit back and hope that referrals will come their way.

The good news is that passive strategies actually work. When they are pleased with your products or services, your customers tell others, and should someone ask for a recommendation, your name is likely to be mentioned.

The better news is that you can improve your access to information, support, and referrals by using a more active strategy. You may find this encouraging; if you're like most entrepreneurs, you'd rather do something to get things moving than sit around waiting for things to happen.

In this chapter we describe eighteen tactics you can use to motivate your Network members. Some of these are direct; that is, you specifically ask for business support or referrals. Others are indirect; they stimulate referrals and support as a result of your taking certain actions. The first fourteen apply primarily to relationship building, the last four directly to referral generation. We will focus our discussion on four aspects of each tactic:

Its purpose or goal. Contacting a source to ask for help can be embarrassing, especially if you haven't been in touch. It's also likely to fail to get results, because your source may feel he is being used. You should make it a point to contact your Network members regularly for other reasons — to offer something of value, such as your help or a business opportunity. By doing so, you gain visibility, respect, and gratitude. When you use one of these tactics to provide a Network source something of value, there's usually an explicit or implicit understanding that you will receive something in return. Your choice of tactics has a major impact on how successful this arrangement will be.

Its benefits. When you contact a source and employ one of these eighteen tactics, you expect to derive certain benefits. Make sure the outcome you expect matches your overall mission.

Its key action steps. Making a tactic work requires planning and following a series of steps. The procedures we have outlined here for each tactic, however, should be considered guidelines, not hard-and-fast rules. Customize these steps to fit your particular situation.

Its applicability and requirements. Some tactics work better with certain kinds of contacts than with others. Our discussion will help you choose the most suitable tactic for approaching each of your contacts.

Volunteering

Purpose

Offering your assistance on a Network member's project or assignment strengthens your cooperative bonds (see also tactic 15, collaborating; tactic 16, sponsoring; and tactic 17, promoting).

Benefits

Helping your Network member achieve an important goal gives you authority to make contact and spend time with him. Besides your initial meeting, you will need to schedule follow-up meetings, receive guidance, get his approval on actions, and provide status reports. The more opportunities he has to observe your follow-through on your commitment, the more he will trust you.

There are two benefits to using this tactic. When your voluntary contributions don't relate to your expertise or business, you are at least establishing trust, reliability, and friendship. When your help comes from your expertise or business, you are also building your business credibility and encouraging future business dealings and referrals.

Steps

- Select your volunteer assignments strategically.
- Investigate what needs to be done before you offer help.
- Offer to spend time, either short term or over a longer period, advising your Network member or helping him achieve a goal or complete a project he is responsible for.
- Provide whatever type of assistance your Network member needs, whether or not it is related to your expertise or business specialty.

Applicability and Requirements

- Set limitations up front on what you have to give and make sure your help is wanted under those conditions.
- Before you commit, make sure you know your target's level of commitment.
- Seek assignments that keep you in contact with your target.
- Look for ways you can help that are easy for you to do but that your target considers high-value support.
- Deliver on your commitments; otherwise, your source may conclude that you can't be depended on.

RECRUITING

Purpose

A prestigious or influential role in your business, whether formal or informal, short term or long term, can mean authority and other benefits for a source. Offer a Network member the opportunity to serve on your board of directors or your advisory board, to make a presentation to an important group, to write an article for a key publication, or to serve as a judge for a contest you are sponsoring.

Benefits

Many people consider it an honor to be asked to assume a key role because it enhances their image as an involved and respected leader. It also lets your sources get to know more about you and other people you know and gives you license to stay in contact with them. This approach will help familiarize your Network members with your business and profession.

Steps

- Identify the roles and assignments you have to offer.
- Identify the individual you want to assume each role.
- Write or call to offer the assignment or role. Describe the role, the time required, the reason the Network member was selected, the benefits the Network member will receive, and a response deadline.

Applicability and Requirements

- Spell out clearly the benefits of being involved.
- Avoid creating a financial obligation for your source, and keep to a minimum the time she needs to invest.
- Let her know that she should accept only if she truly wants to. Encourage her to try it for a while, and let her know that she can quit at any time if it becomes a burden.
- It's best to develop a strong bond of trust before using this approach.

Researching

Purpose

The goal of this tactic is to persuade your Network members to participate in some form of research.

Benefits

This tactic helps you get to know your target market and its needs better. If done well, your research will stimulate your prospective sources' interest in one of your areas of expertise, enhance their knowledge, and generate valuable word of mouth about yourself and your profession. You may even generate new ideas for your business.

Steps

- Design a research project — perhaps a simple survey or a complex questionnaire — on a topic related to your field that you believe will interest your sources.

- Ask your Network members whether they would be willing to participate in some research you are conducting; give them background information about the process, your goals, and how you expect to use the results.

Applicability and Requirements

- Keep your research short, simple, and interesting.

- Since the research approach is one in which you are asking for something from your sources, it is crucial that you follow up with thanks and a summary of the results.

REPORTING

Purpose

Playing the role of reporter is a good way of eliciting information and advice from a Network member — for example, by interviewing him for an article or while doing research on a subject he is familiar with.

Benefits

The reporting approach benefits you in two ways: you learn more about your Network member, and he appreciates the visibility you give him. He will probably be more willing to meet and cooperate with you in other situations, thereby strengthening your relationship. Others will seek you out as an authority or ask you to do articles or research on them. People in business like exposure, especially if it is free.

Steps

- Interview your subject to get information worthy of being publicized — something he is doing or has achieved, or simply his opinion.
- Take pictures of and with your subject when appropriate.
- Publish the information for its largest possible audience in school, church, community, local, or national publications.

Applicability and Requirements

- If appropriate, offer to include your Network member's name in any article or research to which he has contributed information.
- Distribute complimentary copies of your articles or findings to people important to your targets.
- Make no guarantees that what you write will be published.

SOURCE SEEKING

Purpose

This tactic involves contacting your prospective sources to identify people they know who can help you achieve a particular goal. For example, you may ask a source to name someone who

TACTIC

5

- can help you with a problem;
- can sell you something you want;
- owns something you want;
- knows someone in a certain area; or
- has been somewhere you want to go.

Benefits

Using this approach will help you save time and money, increase your number of sources, discover some of your best sources and opportunities, and broaden your knowledge of your sources' networks.

Steps

- Determine what you need; be as clear as possible.
- Identify which sources you will contact for recommendations.
- Contact more than one source for a recommendation; this way, you may find several prospects who can help you with a particular problem.
- Be sure to let your sources know approximately how many options you plan to investigate before you make a final decision.

Applicability and Requirements

- Be aware that some of your sources may be protective about the people in their network. They may want to check with their contacts before they give you their names and numbers.
- Since this approach is primarily one in which your sources give to you, it is important to follow up with thanks and status reports. Be sure to let them know your final decision.

ADVICE SEEKING

Purpose

The purpose of seeking advice is self-explanatory: you need advice, and you ask a Network member for it.

Benefits

People like for others to listen to their opinions and advice. By inviting them to talk, you can get better acquainted with their knowledge, decision-making ability, and attitudes. Receiving someone's advice gives you a reason to contact her again, thank her, and let her know what you plan to do. This is a great way to keep your resources informed and, of course, to get their opinions about what you are doing.

Never ask people for advice without following through by letting them know your decision — whether you follow their recommendations or not. When deciding on the title of his first book, Robert sent several of his associates a list of twelve prospective titles and asked them to identify the three they liked the best. He thanked respondents immediately, in writing. Later he followed through with notes detailing his progress, the target publication date, and his final decision on the title: *Implement Now, Perfect Later: 52 Practical Ways to Increase Gains and Decrease Pains of Perfectionism.*

Steps

- Ask your Network member for advice or opinions on something she enjoys talking about and to which you expect her to have an answer.

- Listen carefully and respond appropriately. Direct your questions toward what your Network member says in conversation; for example, "You made a comment earlier about high-growth investments. What do you think about this no-load fund I've been hearing about?"

Applicability and Requirements

- Have a logical reason for wanting the information.
- Avoid potentially controversial and sensitive issues.
- Don't ask your Network member to give you advice that she would otherwise charge you for.
- People are more likely to remember their own words than others'. If you want someone to remember your conversation, let her do most of the talking.

ADVISING

TACTIC

7

Purpose

This tactic involves giving your prospective sources valuable advice, related to your specialty or profession if possible, such as advance notice of a change in procedures, tips on how to initiate the change, or other information that can help your Network member achieve satisfaction or success (see also tactic 6, advice seeking, and tactic 8, announcing).

Benefits

One of your goals is to get Network members to feel that you are a link to privileged information — that you're an insider. The advice you give may lead your prospective sources to seek you out for answers to their questions or to feel that you're looking out for their best interests. It's a great way to remind your prospective sources of what you do.

Steps

- List the topics that you feel comfortable giving advice on, then list Network members who might need advice on each topic.
- Decide whether you will apply this tactic formally, such as by newsletter, or informally, such as in a personal note.
- Decide how frequently you will send updates.
- Ask your sources to name others who might benefit from your advice.

Applicability and Requirements

- Periodically ask your Network members whether they find your advice useful.
- Tell your Network members to let you know if they don't wish to receive your updates.

ANNOUNCING

TACTIC

8

Purpose

Providing information about upcoming events and opportunities helps make and maintain contacts. The events can be of either business or personal interest, as long as the nature of the function appeals to your audience.

Benefits

Using this approach will cause your audience to view you as an information source and to come to you with questions about other events.

Steps

- Determine what information your Network members would like to have but do not currently receive.
- Identify individuals and groups that value what you have to share.
- When conducting or attending meetings, conferences, or other gatherings, make announcements about upcoming conferences, seminars, shows, meetings, television programs, contests, application deadlines, and other events.
- You can also use this tactic by disseminating written announcements via surface mail, e-mail, or other means.

Applicability and Requirements

- Don't tell people what they already know; the less likely it is that your audience could have heard the information from another source, the better.
- Announce two or three events at a time.
- Don't give away everything in the announcement; ask your audience to contact you individually for details.

Purpose

A good tactic for motivating a Network member is to let her know that you are in the market for her product or service (see also tactic 10, purchasing).

Benefits

Your money is one of your best networking tools. Businesspeople pay a lot of attention to prospective clients and will try to sell you on their products and services. This can lead to greater cooperation and bring opportunities to share information, support, and referrals.

Steps

- Let your prospective source know that you plan to explore a few options before making your purchase.
- Find out from her customers how they are treated.
- Make your purchasing decision within a reasonable time.
- Let her know what factors influenced your decision.

Applicability and Requirements

- Once you've made a purchase, especially a large, one-time purchase such as life insurance or a house, you may find that your source's attention wanes. Therefore, be sure to take full advantage of the attention you get as her prospect.
- Don't apply this tactic to insignificant purchases; buying a tube of toothpaste does not call for a commitment.
- Don't play games; if you're not really interested, don't lead her on.
- Using this approach is definitely a way to test your prospective source's patience and attitude. Does she want to help you meet your needs or just make a quick sale?

PURCHASING

Purpose

One of the friendliest and most natural ways to make contact with a source is to buy his products or services, whether in large or small dollar amounts. The purchase doesn't necessarily have to be from his primary line of business — perhaps a ticket to a fund-raiser, a used car, a computer, even a box of Girl Scout cookies from his daughter.

Benefits

By purchasing something from your Network member, you become one of his customers. As a customer, you are high on his priority list; he will be more inclined to do business with you and give you information, support, and referrals. This approach also increases your source's interest in getting to know you and staying in touch.

Steps

- Analyze how you are spending your money now.
- Decide how much you want to spend.
- Test your relationship with the people you buy from now. Do they know you? Do you benefit from doing business with them?
- Identify the products and services your sources offer that you want or need — or the purchase of which might benefit your business in the long run.

Applicability and Requirements

- Are you buying products and services from people and organizations that see you as an individual? Do the people you buy from know your name and think of you as their customer? There's a big difference between being a customer of Sears and being a customer of Joe's Shoe Store.
- Use your purchasing power in a way that gives you more benefits and builds relationships. Buy at least half of your products and services from people you know; however, don't do it in a way that makes them feel obligated to buy things from you.

CONNECTING

Purpose

Connecting is a tactic designed to help a Network member expand her network of business and personal friends and sources.

TACTIC

11

Benefits

Any help you can give a Network member in achieving success and satisfaction strengthens your bond and enhances your image as a resource-ful, well-connected individual.

Steps

- Introduce your Network member to people who share her interests and who may be able to give her the information, resources, services, support, or inspiration she needs.

- Coordinate your Network member's first meeting with your contact and give them both enough background information to get the relationship off to a quick and productive start.

- In your introduction, include their names, occupations, how you met, the nature of your relationship, a brief description of each person's business, and why each is a person the other should know.

Applicability and Requirements

- It's important to know what kinds of people your prospective source wants to meet; if you're not sure, ask. Likely candidates are people in your target's occupation or contact sphere.

INVITING

Purpose

You can enhance your contact with a prospective source by inviting her to an event you are attending, hosting, or participating in as a featured guest, exhibitor, panel speaker, or award recipient.

Benefits

Inviting them to your events keeps your targets informed of activities you are involved in. When the event is one where you have an opportunity to share your expertise or where you are being recognized for an achievement, using this tactic contributes to building your credibility and image as a successful and knowledgeable professional. This tactic also helps acquaint your targets with others in your Network and transforms strictly business relationships into friendships.

Steps

- Make a list of the events you will be attending and a list of Network members you might invite.
- With plenty of lead time, call or write each prospective source to invite him or her to the event; explain the reason for the invitation.
- Pay your Network member's admission fee, if there is one.

Applicability and Requirements

- Make sure the event offers benefits to your prospective sources, such as an opportunity to meet someone they admire, to be entertained, or to be recognized.
- Whenever possible, allow your guests to invite guests of their own.
- It's okay to invite people you do not expect to attend. Remember, one of your aims is to keep your sources informed of what you are doing.

RECOGNIZING

Purpose

By recognizing your sources for contributing to your business success, you help them both enhance their image and increase their visibility.

Benefits

When others ask your target source about the recognition he has received, it leads to a discussion of his relationship with you or your business and stimulates word of mouth about your sources. It tells other people and sources that someone trusts you, and it makes it easier for them to trust and support you.

Steps

- Publicly compliment, express appreciation, and reward your Network members for their support, leads, referrals, information, and business — for example, with a "customer of the month" contest in which the winner is awarded a certificate, gets his picture posted on a bulletin board, or is written about in a local newspaper.

Applicability and Requirements

- Make sure the recognition and rewards you give are appropriate and that the recipients are worthy.
- Be sincere in your compliments. Share the recognition with the kind of people your prospective sources would like to impress.
- Don't overdo it; extravagant praise may embarrass your target and sound insincere.

HORN TOOTING

TACTIC

Purpose

The idea behind tooting your own horn is to let your sources know about achievements you are proud of.

Benefits

Properly used, this approach will generate interest in you and your business or profession. It should get others to seek you out, ask you questions, and feel that you are knowledgeable and confident. Using this approach may help uncover needs, interests, and achievements that you share with your prospective sources. If you avoid looking like you're just bragging, it will help familiarize others with the services or products you sell.

Along with each year's Christmas card, Robert sends a family holiday letter and a personal note to friends, associates, and clients, keeping them informed of key events and challenges. His 1996 letter mentioned his new role as a director on the board of the National Speakers Association's Los Angeles chapter, an upcoming appearance as the featured guest on a radio talk show, and his soon-to-be-available book. On the back of the letter was printed Robert Valett's "ABCs of Happiness" (below). This horn tooting brought in several calls and a few book orders.

The ABCs of Happiness

Aspire to reach your potential. **B**elieve in yourself. **C**reate a good life. **D**ream about what you might become. **E**xercise frequently. **F**orgive honest mistakes. **G**lorify the creative spirit. **H**umor yourself and others. **I**magine great things. **J**oyfully live each day. **K**indly help others. **L**ove one another. **M**editate daily. **N**urture the environment. **O**rganize for harmonious action. **P**raise performance well done. **Q**uestion most things. **R**egulate your own behavior. **S**mile often. **T**hink rationally. **U**nderstand yourself. **V**alue life. **W**ork for the common good. **X**-ray and carefully examine problems. **Y**earn to improve. **Z**estfully pursue happiness.

By Robert Valett

Steps

- During everyday conversations, phone calls, and introductions, casually keep your sources informed about your achievements, plans, assets, and networks.

- You can also do a little low-key horn tooting through e-mail or other correspondence.

Applicability and Requirements

- Remember, your purpose is not to brag; rather, you want to share with your sources, in a modest way, some of the things you've achieved.

COLLABORATING

Purpose

The collaborating tactic is used to express interest in establishing an informal partnership with a contact for your mutual benefit.

Benefits

One of the best ways to obtain a commitment from a Network member is to make a commitment to share resources and efforts. Collaborating creates a reliable and committed source of information, support, and referrals and helps you achieve your goals more easily and quickly.

In producing their audiocassette program, *Total Quality Introductions*, Robert's collaboration with Laura Miller helped them get a good start. Neither of them had a product, but they knew that developing products could significantly enhance their success as trainers and speakers. They shared costs, time, and resources; they encouraged each other; their relationship grew stronger. It took about a year, but they got the tape done much sooner than they would have by doing it alone. Since that project they have individually produced other tapes and products, but it was the initial collaboration that got them off the ground.

Steps

- Decide on what kinds of resources you need to obtain — information, support, or referrals.
- Select a prospective source.
- Meet with the source to discuss the type of partnership, your needs and resources, and her needs and resources.
- Frame an informal agreement on how the partnership will work — what resources you will share, how you will share them, and for how long.

Applicability and Requirements

- You and your partner must be very clear about what you want and expect from each other. Select someone you trust, someone who will pursue goals with as much energy as you.
- If you can, set up a trial collaboration before you establish a long-term commitment.

Sponsoring

Purpose

The purpose of sponsoring is to help your sources by providing financial and resource backing for projects or programs they are involved with.

Benefits

Sponsoring a program or event gives you an opportunity to work with sources and prospective customers for a definite period. When you sponsor an event or activity, you usually communicate with many people through correspondence, personal introductions, promotional literature, signs, and banners. By doing so, you gain exposure to potential customers or influential individuals in your target market, people who can provide business support and referrals. Other benefits, such as display and distribution of your promotional materials, can be negotiated.

Steps

- Select an organization or individual you want to sponsor.
- Decide how you wish to benefit the company.
- Negotiate the benefits.

Applicability and Requirements

- It's important to select a project or program that suits your beliefs, values, philosophy, and goals.
- Use this approach with sources who have a strong relationship with individuals and organizations in one of your target markets.

PROMOTING

Purpose

This tactic is designed to get information, support, and referrals by providing promotional support to your sources; to demonstrate to them how well you know them and trust them; and to help build relationships between them and other members of your Network. Because this is an indirect approach, there's no guarantee that you'll receive promotional support and referrals in return.

TACTIC

17

Benefits

Helping your sources get business makes them more likely to help you get business. By letting them know exactly what actions you have taken on their behalf, you give them a model for generating business for you.

Steps

- Introduce a member of your Network to another member or acquaintance. Describe your Network member's background and business and how well she performs.

- Let the other person know that if he ever needs the kind of products or services offered by your Network member, he should not hesitate to call on her.

- Promote your Network member as often as possible, whether or not she is present — for example, by nominating her for an award or using her as an example in presentations and introductions.

Applicability and Requirements

- Be selective with this approach, and truthful about your Network members; you don't think the world of everyone.

- Don't make your sources feel obligated because you have promoted them or generated business for them.

- Be patient, continue to give strategically, and the business support and referrals you want will come.

AUDITING

Purpose

Auditing is a two-tiered tactic. Initially, its purpose is to obtain feedback and suggestions from clients and observers on their experience with your products and services. If the information you receive is positive, contact your sources again to solicit their involvement in some of your promotional activities or to request permission to use their feedback in your promotional campaign.

Benefits

Using this approach will help you identify your true believers and champions. You'll generate ideas on how to make things better and you'll capture clients' opinions in writing. This approach will help you discover new opportunities and spot problems early. Most important, it will help you generate testimonial statements, endorsements, and referrals.

Steps

- Design an oral or written survey or questionnaire.
- Identify the group you will survey.
- Get feedback from your sources on the quality of your products and services by conducting surveys during or immediately after delivery of your service or product.

Applicability and Requirements

- Use this approach with sources who have firsthand knowledge of your products or services, and get their feedback as close to the delivery point as possible.
- Be sure to let your sources know how you used their feedback.

Choosing the Best Tactics

OU NOW HAVE THE OUTLINES of eighteen tactics that you can use to cause your Network members to want to provide you with information, support, and referrals. Your decision on which to use, and with which sources, depends on the situation, your personal and professional style, and the results you expect to achieve.

● *TACTICS: In component 6 of your Referral Marketing Plan (appendix B), list the motivational tactics you consider most appropriate for you, your business, and your Referral Network members. Describe how you would adapt them for your own best use.*

Part

V

Activating Your Referral Network

Part	Chapter	Referral Marketing Plan Component	
I	1		
	2		
II	3	1. Mission Statement	41
	4	2. Products and Services	42
	5	3. Target Market	43
III	6	4. Competition	45
	7		
	8		
	9		
	10		
IV	11	5. Matching Needs and Prospective Sources	93
	12	6. Tactics	115
V	13		
	14	7. Referral Marketing System	123, 132, 144
	15		
	16	8. Time Budget	149
	17	9. Calendar	152
VI	18	10. Cost Budget	154
	19	11. Sales and Referral Projections	160
	20	12. Tracking and Evaluation	171

Recruiting Referral Sources

Getting Your Network Members on Board

ET'S ASSUME you've applied one or more of the techniques described in the last chapter and have received a referral — better yet, lots of referrals. What do you do next? Just sit back and watch the money roll in? No, you've still got lots of work to do.

Getting referrals is great; however, until your prospect makes a purchase, you're looking at only potential business. The true success of your efforts is measured by the number of referrals that you convert into customers. That's what this chapter and the four that follow will show you how to do — generate referrals and turn them into customers and business opportunities.

Our method of generating and using referrals has five phases:

- recruiting the prospective referral source;
- briefing the referral source;
- priming the prospect (source's action);
- initiating contact with the prospect; and
- rewarding your referral source.

These are the five phases involved in activating your referral network. Familiarize yourself with all five phases before you begin; you'll find it a lot easier to understand and apply the method. This chapter describes the first of these phases, recruiting the referral source.

ACTIVE, NOT PASSIVE

THE ONLY WAY to generate referrals is through other people. Although this five-phase method can work with new and developing relationships, it is designed to be used primarily with strong relationships — people with whom you share a strong common interest over a long period.

The heart of the method is active, not passive, recruitment. You can, of course, put the system in motion the moment someone tells you she knows someone who may need your products or services. But don't wait around for referrals; go find them. The more high-quality referrals you can generate, the better your business.

You should recruit referral sources who

- want or can be inspired to help you;
- have time or are willing to make the time to help you;
- have the ability or can be trained to do the things you want them to do;
- have the resources necessary to help you;
- have relationships with the types of people you want to target; and
- would make good referrals for people you know.

If you've understood the book thus far, and if you've completed the worksheets, you've already done most of the work necessary for turning referrals into business. You've selected prospective referral sources. To strengthen your relationships with them, you've learned more about their GAINS and better acquainted them with yours. You've thought about the specific kinds of help you'll need from them. And although a strong relationship with them is by itself one of the best referral generators, you've decided to use other tactics as well. One of the best ways to motivate your sources is to offer them help in using this referral-generating system to get their own customers and business opportunities.

> *One of the best ways to motivate your sources is to offer them help in using this referral-generating system to get their own customers and business opportunities.*

INITIAL CONTACT

AFTER YOU'VE COMPILED your list of excellent prospective referral sources, your next action is to begin contacting them. What's the best way to get your message to them? Should you send them a letter, e-mail or fax them, or arrange to meet them in person? Any of these formats could work; however, your first communication with a prospective source is best done by phone. It's more personal and friendly than a written message, but it is more convenient for both you and your source than a face-to-face meeting.

Before you call, plan your call carefully. Decide which topics you want to cover. Remember, the purpose of your call is to ask for support in generating referrals, to give a brief overview of your plans, and to schedule an appointment to discuss your plans in detail. Here are a few guidelines:

- Begin with an appropriate greeting and small talk.
- State the purpose of your call and the amount of time you need.
- Ask whether this is a good time to talk.
- Get into the heart of your conversation by offering the person you are calling something of value. For example, explain how the topics you want to cover will help him.

121

- Tell your prospective source that you'd like to have his help in generating referrals for your business and ask for a meeting to discuss the details.

- Schedule a face-to-face meeting or a telephone conference.

- Tell him you have some information for him to review (this will be covered in the next chapter).

SCRIPTING YOUR CALL

ALTHOUGH YOU SHOULDN'T expect to follow it mechanically, you may find it useful to prepare a script to anticipate how your first contact may go. To show you how to do this, we'll invent a fictional character, Dr. Mark Star, whose goal is to recruit a referral source, Trudy Grossman, who might help him secure a radio talk show interview with her friend Ethel Clearchannel to promote his new book.

Greeting: "Hi, Trudy."

Small talk: "How are you doing? . . . How's your family? . . . Did you go anywhere over the weekend?"

Purpose: "Trudy, the reason I'm calling is to see if you can help me get a radio talk show interview to promote my new book. And I'd also like to show you how I can help you generate referrals for your business. Right now I'd like to give you a quick overview of some ideas I have and get your reaction to them. Is this a good time? If you're interested, we can arrange to discuss them later in more detail." (If yes, continue.)

Overview: "As I'm sure you know, getting referrals is one of the best ways to generate business. I've been reading about a systematic approach for generating referrals that was developed by Dr. Ivan Misner and Robert Davis, and I've prepared a plan that will help me attract more customers and business opportunities. It's practical, and I believe it covers everything. If you're interested, I'd like to show you how to use the system for your business, too. Are you interested?" (If yes, continue.)

Scheduling the meeting: "Great! I'd like to meet with you as soon as possible — say, within the next week or two — to tell you my ideas. It should take about an hour. When would be the best time for you?"

Close: "Okay, Trudy, I'll send you an outline of what we need to discuss and some information that will help you understand how the system works. You should get it in a day or two. If you have any questions before we meet, please don't hesitate to call. It was great talking with you. I look forward to our meeting on _____ at _____."

COMPLETING THE FIRST PHASE

BASED ON THE GUIDELINES and sample script, develop an outline that you can use for your initial contact with your prospective sources. After you've reviewed the remaining four phases of this activation process, you can fine-tune your script and begin making calls.

● *REFERRAL MARKETING SYSTEM: As you recruit each new member of your Referral Network, add your source's name to component 7 of your Referral Marketing Plan (appendix B).*

Chapter 14

Briefing Your Sources

Training Your Network Members to Send Referrals

U PON GETTING A BUSINESS REFERRAL, Mr. John Q. Businessman simply takes down the name and contact information of the potential customer, Arlene D. Prospect, from the referral source. Sometime later, he calls the prospect and introduces himself: "Hello, Ms. Prospect, my name is John Businessman. Larry Source recommended I call you. I'm an accountant. . . ."

Handling referrals this way, as you might expect, gets minimal results. Your chance of converting the referral into a customer will be greater if your referral source

- makes the initial contact with the prospect (his acquaintance) to assess her need and, if appropriate, alert her that you will be getting in touch;
- sends the prospect background information about you and your business;
- lets the prospect know the nature of his relationship with you;
- gives the prospect a brief description and endorsement of your products or services;
- arranges to introduce the prospect to you; and
- follows up with the prospect after you contact her.

Unfortunately, if you don't ask your prospective referral source to do some of these things, he probably won't — not because he isn't willing, but because he doesn't know these actions could make a big difference, doesn't have enough information about you or your business, or simply doesn't know how.

A Plan for Your Source

THERE ARE TWO MAIN ACTIONS you need to take: (1) communicate to your sources the actions you wish them to take, and (2) provide them with all materials necessary to accomplish those actions. More specifically, it is your responsibility to your prospective referral sources to

- prepare an agenda for a briefing session;
- show them how they can help you generate referrals and convert them into customers;
- develop sample correspondence and literature for them;
- prepare outlines and scripts that they can use when making contact with prospects;
- give them clear instructions on what you want them to do for you;
- provide typing and other administrative support;

- pay all expenses they incur on your behalf, including postage, telephone calls, and promotional materials; and
- make it as easy as possible for them to support you.

Exactly how do you meet these responsibilities? There are four steps to briefing a prospective referral source:

Step 1: When you make your first call asking for help, give your prospective referral source a brief overview of your approach to getting referrals (see chapter 13).

Step 2: Before your first meeting, send your prospective source a packet of information and materials (as you promised in your phone call), including

- a comprehensive agenda for the briefing session (see "Sample Agenda," p. 128),
- a description of the source's role and yours (see "Roles," p. 128),
- sample outlines, scripts, and other materials, and
- a Business Referral Tool (appendix A-17).

You should call before your first meeting to be sure your prospective source has received these materials. Remind him to take a look at the materials; you can do this by asking whether he has any questions about them. Your training session will go faster and more smoothly if he has read the materials ahead of time.

Note that the Business Referral Tool is a record that you maintain for your own purposes; you should not ask your prospective source to fill it out for you (although a source with whom you have a close relationship might volunteer to do so). However, be sure to point out the potential value of this tool for your source's own referral marketing.

Step 3: Conduct referral source education and training. Each session can be formal or informal, a one-on-one meeting or a class lesson for several sources at once — whatever fits your situation, your style, and your prospective sources' needs. For at least the first session, you should be the person conducting the training. Later, you may find that some of your better referral sources can be very effective in helping you train new sources. The responsibility for all training costs is yours, of course.

This step, briefing your prospective sources, is the heart of the process; don't do it haphazardly. Your goal is to teach your sources how to carry out the roles they will play in helping you generate referrals and convert them into customers.

Sample Agenda

Introduction

Thanks

Purpose of meeting:

- Explain how you can help me generate referrals and convert them into clients
- Teach you what you need to know to act as a referral source
- Provide the tools you need to carry out your role as a referral source
- Finalize a plan of action

Overview of agenda

Review of support materials mailed

Business development goals:

- Overview of my products and services
- Target market

Benefits to be gained

Advantages of using the five-phase system

How the five-phase system works:

- Definitions
- Prerequisites
- The five phases

Other ways to provide support

How the system can be used to help you

Recommended plan of action

Questions and answers

Finalization of action plan

Conclusion

Roles

My role (partial list)

Before the meeting:

- Select target market
- Identify desired help

During meeting:

- Develop and provide training for you
- Provide you with complimentary samples of products and services

After meeting:

- Provide you with required support materials and funds to pay for all expenses, including postage and telephone calls

Your role (partial list)

- Collect and provide information about prospects
- Contact prospect before contacting me
- Give prospect background information and promote my products and services
- Send information packet to prospect

Review with your source the materials you sent. Be thorough and quick. Try to limit your training to an hour or two; if you need more time, spread it over several days. The more your referral sources know about you, your business, and what they can do to assist you, the better — but don't use up too much of their valuable time.

Step 4: Provide the referral source with follow-up materials, information, and support as needed. Continue the training via telephone conversations and additional briefings and debriefings, especially after his first few calls to prospects. This will enable your referral sources to

- help you collect key information that you could not have obtained on your own;

- better understand your products or services and communicate their value to others; and

- answer key questions about you and your products or services.

To train his referral resources, Robert conducted a morning and an afternoon session at a hotel in Ontario, California. He devoted some of the time to getting his associates acquainted with one another. During each session, which lasted about three hours and was attended by about twelve people, Robert gave participants the following information:

- a description of the program he was offering,

- a list of ways they could help him, and

- a list of ways he could help them.

The sessions were a major success. They were a great way for Robert to get the support he needed and to increase his associates' awareness of him, his business, and how he could contribute to their success. He also received an invitation to appear on a radio talk show, a roster of prospective contacts, a list of some of the needs of his sources, and much more. He plans to offer another session within the year.

Right now you're probably thinking, Whoa, I could never expect my referral sources to do all these things for me. A sit-down training session would take much more time than they have available, and the amount of work I'm asking them to do would make them feel like unpaid employees.

Remember the conditions we set earlier: this process applies only to people with whom you have a long, strong relationship, a high level of trust, or an agreement to perform services for each other for your mutual benefit. In effect, these people are informal business partners with you; you have agreed to perform unpaid services for each other that will help your respective businesses. Often this informal agreement has been made in an organizational setting, such as a referral service organization.

If it has not already been explicitly agreed to, tell your prospective source that you wish to share with him the process you are using to generate referral business. Tell him exactly what you are doing, in terms of both your business mission and the means you use to obtain new customers, and that you wish to learn the same things about his business. The results you expect are twofold: (1) he will send you new referral business, and (2) he will improve his referral-generating process and get referral business from you.

THE SHORT COURSE

YOU WILL FIND YOURSELF in many relationships that fall short of the close, trusting kind needed for the formal training sessions described above. In fact, you may get occasional referrals from people you haven't even met. Between these extremes, however, is a broad range of relationships that call for different ways of imparting information about yourself and your products or services that can be passed along to prospects. Many of the motivational tactics outlined in chapter 12 also serve, in part, as a form of training for your referral source.

Here are several ways, both formal and informal, to provide your sources useful information about your products or services — information they can pass along to prospects that may result in referral business:

- Ask your prospective source to critique your marketing materials, such as your flyers, brochures, videos, audiotapes, even your résumé. Send them your drafts, not the finished product. As they offer advice on how to improve the item, they will learn more about your business and remember more facts about you.

- Send them your newsletter. In it you can describe activities your sources may not be familiar with. They can pass this information, or even the entire newsletter, to people who might want to do business with you.

- Ask your source to introduce you for a presentation you are going to make. Your source will want more information about you in order to make a good introduction. Promise to help her by providing her with notes.

- Tell your friends and associates, especially new ones, you want to get to know them better. Ask for information about their jobs, professions, interests, organizations, networks, and hobbies. At the same time, give them a profile of yourself — including a picture, to remind those you haven't seen in a while what you look like.

- Invite your sources to attend events at which they can learn more about you — an award ceremony, an open house, a trade show, a social function. Make sure they learn something about you from the invitation itself. If you sponsor the event but are not the main attraction, try to devote a few minutes after the main presentation to describing your business. Merrill Lynch financial consultants often sponsor lunchtime speakers and use the opportunity for an additional brief presentation of their services.

- Record information about yourself in your answering machine message. One businessman uses this message: "Thanks for calling Chesney Communications. We produce the business television program 'Windows on Wall Street.' If you're calling about our duplication services, press 22; our video production services, press 30. For all other departments, press 0."

- Invite a source to speak to your group about something she does or knows. This will lead her to ask for facts about you and your organization.

- Invite sources to visit your web page. Send them a note announcing your new web page and ask them to provide feedback. Make

---

One specialty book publisher finds most of his new authors by referrals from other authors whose books he has published. To help cut down the number of inappropriate referrals (topics outside his specialty), he publishes and distributes a free newsletter. Each of his published authors, as well as book buyers and others in the field, receive the newsletter every few months.

Each issue describes upcoming books, their subject matter, their expected audience, and the authors' and publisher's marketing plans. In other sections are lists of the publisher's books in print, total sales, comments and quotes from reviews, bestseller lists the books have made, and other news from the publisher.

With the first issue the publisher mails to each new subscriber, he includes a cover letter stating the purpose of the newsletter: to keep readers informed of events in the book business, and to help publicize and market each author's book. He encourages the reader to tell other potential authors about his business, his preferred topics, and the special services and high-quality product he offers. In this way, he is able to both increase his desirable referrals and cut down on the number of undesirable ones.

The publisher's newsletter helps him in several ways: it spreads the word about his products and services, pleases his established customers by spotlighting their books, and — not least — improves the quality of his referral-generated business.

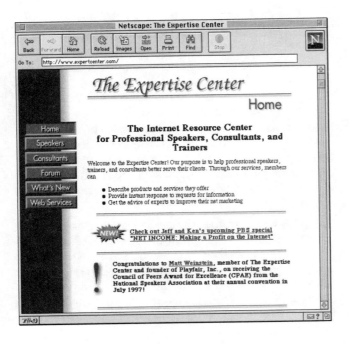

sure it offers information that will help them understand your business.

- At the end of your e-mail messages, after your name, include a "sig" file that lists information such as nicknames, positions you hold, books you've written, and special recognition you've received. Limit your list to 10 lines. Change your sig periodically so that regular correspondents can learn more about you.

- Ask your source for advice. Give him plenty of background information to help him formulate his recommendations.

GETTING TO KNOW YOU

A S WE LEARNED in the GAINS approach (chapter 11), getting acquainted with your sources is a two-way street. You need to know about your prospective source in order to gauge the kind of prospect she is likely to send you and work within the framework of her business or profession. She needs to know about you in order to select good prospects for your products or services and to recommend your strengths and specialties to them.

- **BRIEFING YOUR SOURCES: Continue filling in component 7 of your Referral Marketing Plan (appendix B) by deciding how you will brief each member of your Referral Network.**

When the benefits come through, it's still a two-way street. Make sure the source of a good referral can benefit from your actions in return for her help to you. There are several ways of accomplishing this, as you will see in later chapters.

Chapter 15

Priming Your Prospects

Your Source's First Contact on Your Behalf

THE THIRD PHASE of activating your Referral Network has the most significant impact on your success in converting referrals into customers — and it's the only action in the process that's not yours to take. It is your referral source's responsibility to make the first contact with your prospect (her acquaintance) — to tell him he'll be hearing from you. There's a good reason for this. The prospect is more likely to talk with you, purchase your product or service, or provide a business opportunity if he learns about you from someone he trusts.

He's even more likely to do so if your source first does a little research into whether he might need, want, or be interested in your product or service, and if she then completes a Business Referral worksheet for you. If your referral source learns that the prospect can benefit from your business, she tells him about you; if not, she simply doesn't mention you.

BE INQUISITIVE

PERHAPS THE BEST WAY for your source to assess the prospect is to ask questions, and she's usually better positioned to get the answers than you are. For example, Dr. Star's referral source, Trudy Grossman, can ask the prospect (her friend Ethel Clearchannel, the radio show host) questions such as these:

- How do you select guests for your show? Who makes the final decision?
- What kind of topics do you like to cover?
- What topics do you plan to cover during the next few months?
- Are you open to suggestions? Would you be interested in some referrals?
- What dates are you trying to fill?

Once your source tells you how the prospect responded to her questions, you'll have a better idea of how to approach her when your turn comes. Then, when the time is right and circumstances are favorable, ask your source to alert the prospect that you'll be getting in touch.

Robert's friend Laura Miller suggested that he contact Ingrid, with the *Empire Business Journal*, about the possibility of speaking to the *Journal*'s annual women's conference. Robert asked Laura first to tell Ingrid that he would be a good speaker for the conference and that she was going to ask Robert to call. Laura agreed.

She called Robert back the same day. Ingrid had already selected the speakers for the conference, she said, but there was another possibility; he should call Ingrid right away. Robert did so, and before he finished introducing himself, Ingrid said, "Oh, yeah. Hi, Robert. I was expecting your call. Are you available for a radio show interview next Wednesday?" Laura's help with the prospect had turned a tough sell into a real business opportunity.

FOLLOW THROUGH

AFTER YOUR SOURCE TALKS with the prospect, she should follow up in writing. This gives the prospect an opportunity to learn more about you before you make contact — or serves as a reminder if the prospect has forgotten what the source said about you. This follow-up should include a cover letter and some brochures or other literature describing your background and business — materials that you have thoughtfully provided your source (in the second phase).

Here's an example of a follow-up letter from a referral source to a prospect — in this case, Dr. Mark Star's source Trudy Grossman, to her friend Ethel, the talk show host:

> October 30, 1997
>
> Hi, Ethel,
>
> It was great talking with you. Congratulations on your nomination to VP of your community organization. I am delighted that things are going well with you.
>
> The materials I promised to send you on Dr. Mark Star are enclosed. As I mentioned, Mark would be an excellent guest for your show. He recently appeared on "Making It" on KYPA and talked about strategies for achieving goals. As usual, Mark was lively, professional, and very informative. Here's a copy of his brochure for your review.
>
> If you have no objections, I will ask Mark to give you a call next week.
>
> See you at the breakfast meeting next month.
>
> Trudy Grossman
> cc: Dr. Mark Star

PROVIDE FEEDBACK

FINALLY, THE REFERRAL SOURCE should let you know what's happened. She can do this by phone, e-mail, fax, or other means, or, as in the example, by forwarding to you a copy of her letter to the prospect. Make sure she lets you know who is expected to make the next move, and when.

This may seem like a lot to ask of a referral source — but remember, you are handling most of the behind-the-scenes work that makes the system effective. In addition, your referral source derives several benefits from helping you:

- the opportunity to contact an acquaintance for reasons other than her own business needs;
- a stronger relationship with the prospect;
- the chance to look like a hero for offering a referral with no expectation of monetary reward;
- a commitment from you, the vendor, to reciprocate by helping her secure referrals for her business; and
- being viewed as a source.

Thus, getting support from a referral source works in the best interests of both of you. More important, working with your referral source will yield far greater results than working alone.

Chapter 16

Contacting Your Prospects

Your First Communication with Your Future Client

YOUR REFERRAL SOURCE has done her job. Now it's time to contact the prospect. But be careful: the purpose of your first contact is not to make a sale or even to ask the prospect if he has questions about your business. If — and only if — the prospect asks should you present your products or services during this contact.

The purpose of the initial contact with the prospect is

- to begin to build the relationship;
- to get to know the prospect better;
- to help the prospect get to know you better;
- to position yourself to make your next contact; and
- to see if the prospect fits your source's description of her.

Before making contact, do your homework. If you don't have them, ask for copies of all correspondence your source sent the prospect on your behalf. Review your Business Referral tool. Find out from your source the best way to make your initial contact — telephone? letter? e-mail?

MEET THE FACE

WHEN YOUR SOURCE gives you the green light, don't let the opportunity grow stale. Make your first contact with the prospect within 72 hours. If your source can be present, the most advantageous way is a face-to-face meeting in which your source can introduce you. This introduction should be more than just "Harry, this is Jerry. Jerry, this is Harry"; your source should give the prospect a more thorough briefing about you, your business, and your products or services. For example:

"Harry Prospect, this is Vic Vendor, whom I was telling you about last week at our club meeting. Vic and I have known each other for more than five years. For the last two years, I've let him handle all my travel arrangements, and I can't count up all the dollars he's saved me, not to mention bench time in airport lounges. Vic's really active in the community; we're going to give him our service award at our next chamber meeting. He's also a good golfer and he skis a lot in the winter, although I find that hard to believe because he's never broken a leg.

"Vic, Harry's been a very special customer of mine for at least fifteen years. His daughter and mine went to school together, and he let me cater her wedding three years ago. . . ." And so forth.

During your first contact, the prospect will be watching to see whether you are as enthusiastic, caring, articulate, straightforward, and intelligent as your source said you were. He may have questions, but typically will not ask them during the first meeting unless he has an urgent need for the kind of products or services you provide.

DROP A LINE

F YOUR FIRST MEETING with your prospect can't be in person, your best bet is to write — a letter, a card, or e-mail, for example — rather than to phone, as you did your prospective source. Writing gives you a better, more controlled opportunity to convey what you've learned about the prospect. It helps develop your relationship to let your prospect know you find him interesting enough to have taken the time to learn a few facts about him — not the fact that he needs your products or services, but the fact that he's a member of the Downtown Executive Society, or that "Tom told me you're a great chess player." Express an interest in meeting him. Advise him that you'll be calling to schedule a mutually convenient appointment. Don't expect him to have read, or to remember, the materials your source sent him.

Start by naming your referral source — a name he will recognize:

> Dear Glen:
>
> Joan Irvine, who I understand was one of your students, recommended that I get in touch with you. Joan tells me that you are an avid butterfly collector . . .

Don't send business literature or your card with your first correspondence. Your stationery should have all the contact information your prospect needs to reach you. Avoid giving the impression that you are interested in him primarily as a prospective customer.

If your prospect will agree, schedule a meeting. Regardless, offer to send more information, and if the prospect indicates he would like this, do so right away (and don't forget to send a copy of your correspondence to your referral source).

RING UP

F YOUR SOURCE RECOMMENDS it and can guide you as to the best time to do so, you can contact your prospect by telephone:

"Hello, Ms. Clearchannel, I'm Dr. Mark Star, and I'm calling you at the recommendation of Trudy Grossman."

"Oh, hi, Mark. Trudy told me about you. She's quite impressed with your book. I'd like to have you on my show. Can you come to my studio two weeks from today?"

The above situation could happen, of course: the prospect could decide immediately to do business with you. If you've prepared the ground well, and if you're lucky, your efforts may pay off on your very first call. Most often, though, the prospect — even a referred lead — will need more time or express an interest in talking later about your products or services. However, you're almost certainly better off than if you made your first contact by cold call, mass advertising, or direct-mail campaign.

FOLLOW UP

WHEN BUILDING RELATIONSHIPS, it's always important not to let much time lapse without following up the first contact. Within seventy-two hours, send your prospect a note expressing your pleasure in communicating with her. It's still too early, though, to send business literature or make any move toward sales promotion.

Follow up early, but don't push beyond the prospect's comfort level. Once the prospect has expressed an interest in your products or services, provide information about them, but don't force it on her. Continue presenting your products or services, but avoid the hard sell. Focus on fulfilling her needs and interests. Your goal should be to keep your prospect aware of your business without annoying her.

Remember, to secure the long-term loyalty of your prospect and convert her into a customer, you must first build a relationship, and that relationship must develop through the visibility, credibility, and profitability stages. It may take a while, but if you've selected and briefed your sources well, and if you use this five-phase action model to its best advantage, you'll speed up the process.

Chapter 17

Recognizing and Rewarding Your Sources

*Providing Feedback
and Incentives to
Your Network Members*

THE FINAL PHASE in activating your Referral Network is to keep your referral source apprised of what has happened since she gave you the referral, and to show your appreciation. It's important to recognize and reward your source — both before and certainly after a referral has become a customer. This chapter will show you how to set up two important parts of this process: a system for sharing results and a system for recognizing and rewarding referral sources.

SHARE RESULTS

BE SURE TO SHARE your results regularly and systematically with your referral sources. First, determine the kinds of information about results you want to share, then set up a method of capturing this information. It should come from the data you collected on the Business Referral Tool. If it doesn't, modify the form. Next, determine how you will share the results — that is, by phone, e-mail, fax, card, or letter. Whatever the means, always

- give your referral source a brief update on what has happened;
- share what you plan to do next; and
- promise to keep her informed.

This third point is important. You want your referral source to expect to hear from you regularly. Your promise sets up that expectation; it obligates you to keep in touch, and you must keep your promises. Your relationship must develop beyond visibility into credibility before you can expect to reach profitability. You can reinforce your credibility by saying, "I promised to keep you informed of my situation, so here's my news." But remember: failure to keep this promise will damage your credibility.

To reinforce the relationship, call or write your source to talk about something other than the prospect. Pass along news about your personal or professional life and ask about hers. Now and then, send a small, thoughtful gift or complimentary offering — an inspirational message, a product sample, an article, a piece of your newest literature.

You will derive many benefits from sharing your results with your referral source. Doing so

- increases your likelihood of getting additional support. Informing your source of your plans gives her an opportunity to support or advise you and keeps the information pipeline open;
- keeps your name in front of the prospect and your referral source, keeps your source and prospect in touch with each other, and increases your chances of being remembered by both. You can bet that when your referral source and prospect get together they will talk about your situation;

- strengthens your relationship with the referral source, because each update includes yet another expression of gratitude. People like to be thought of as helpful; and

- enhances your source's knowledge of you and your business. Sharing your results contributes to her education, increasing her confidence in you and her ability to spot prospective customers for your business.

CREATE A REWARD PROGRAM

O SHARE REWARDS equitably and effectively, you must do so predictably. This requires being explicit and systematic in your reward philosophy. If you sometimes reward certain actions and sometimes not, your sources will consider you ungrateful or unreliable. To establish a consistent reward program that provides incentive for your sources, you need to decide

- when to reward a source — upon receipt of a good referral, or when the deal is closed?

- what kind of reward — gift, cash, finder's fee?

- how much you can afford — what's the best gift you can offer within your budget?

- what kind of reward your sources would value most — and probably not buy for themselves.

- when and how the reward will be presented.

- how you will keep track of your reward activity.

ONE FREE HOUR

Like everything else about Special Graphics, this certificate is valuable. It is worth One **FREE** Hour of advertising and marketing consultation time to you or your referral. It can only be used once and has no expiration date. It is our way of introducing Special Graphics and our special way of positioning valuable products or services to be in the best interest of their markets.

Richard Feldman, Partner/Business & Sales

Special Graphics

3 Spohia Drive
West Nyack, NY 10994
sg ads@aol.com :eMail
914.353.1725 :Ph
914.353.3976 :Fx

It's good practice to develop a list of ways to reward referral sources. Distinguish between tangible (e.g., cash) and intangible (e.g., a public "thank you") rewards. Estimate the cost and set aside funds to pay for your recognition program. The key is to find a unique, memorable way to say thank you and to encourage your colleagues and friends to keep sending you referrals that turn into business. One small-business owner sends a fine Waterman pen, with a personal note of thanks, to each colleague who makes a referral that leads to a sale. The sidebar "Business Associates Referral Program" illustrates how another company rewards its referral sources with a one-time credit toward purchases of its products and services.

Once a referral has become a customer, be sure to recognize and reward your source appropriately. Doing so encourages her to send you more referrals. It increases her confidence that you can deliver on your promises. When she tells prospects about you, she will have good things to say about your integrity and the quality of your work.

It may take a while, but if you've selected and trained your sources well, and if you use the system to its best advantage, you will speed up the process of turning referrals into business.

Business Associates Referral Program

You can save hundreds of dollars by participating in our Business Associates Referral Program. Here's how it works:

Referred Customer Bills:	You Receive:
$51–$100 monthly	$25 one-time credit
$101+ monthly	$100 one-time credit

The billing period that the program is based on is the first two months. If the customer has paid the invoice, the higher qualifying month will determine the credit you receive.

● **REWARDING YOUR SOURCES:** Complete component 7 of your Referral Marketing Plan (appendix B) by choosing the reward tactic or tactics you consider most appropriate to use with each member of your Referral Network.

Part

VI

Managing Your Referrals

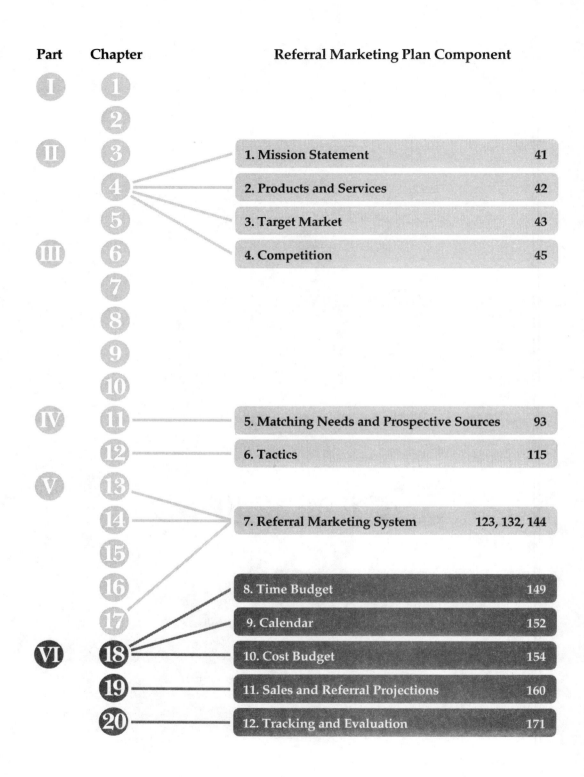

Chapter 18

Budgeting for Referrals

Allocating Your Time and Your Money

SYSTEMATIC REFERRAL MARKETING requires planning. You need to budget the time and money you'll need for your Referral Marketing Campaign (RMC). In this chapter we will outline a step-by-step approach you can use, and several considerations you need to be aware of, in budgeting your time. Then we will describe a similar approach for your expenses.

BUDGETING AND ALLOCATING YOUR TIME

EVERY BUSINESS PLAN should include estimates of how long it will take and how the time will be used. Before implementing your RMC, check to see if you will have enough time to carry out your plans. If you don't know this, you risk, among other things,

- spending too much or too little time on a particular effort;
- losing control of your time;
- realizing little or no return on your investment of time; or
- abandoning your efforts too soon.

In our systematic approach to budgeting time, we've identified seven steps. All that you need to do to complete component 8 of your Referral Marketing Plan is the first two steps; you'll also need to do step 7 to schedule contacts on your master calendar (component 9). If you prefer a more detailed approach, you can do steps 3 through 6 as well.

Step 1: Estimate Total Time Available

Your campaign can be as long as you want it to be — three, six, nine, twelve months or more. Within those constraints, how much time do you wish to devote to your RMC? Will you need 100, 200, 350, or 500 hours? The time you have available — that you reserve — will determine the nature and quality of your RMC by influencing your selection of tactics, objectives, resources, targets, and so forth.

To estimate the time you will need, use whatever information you can from your past experience and the experiences of others, such as your Network members. About how much time did you spend last year on developing relationships and networking? If no such information is available, make an educated guess for your first campaign, then adjust using this initial experience as a guide.

Your time estimate can be a daily, weekly, monthly, quarterly, or annual figure. Our example will span twelve months, and we will allocate 120 hours to our six selected referral sources.

Step 2: Estimate Total Time Available per Period

Allocate the available time, 120 hours in our example, by month. Let's assume our business is seasonal, and that we will have less time available for networking in the summer and the holiday season.

	Month											
	1	2	3	4	5	6	7	8	9	10	11	12
Hours:	12	12	12	12	10	8	8	8	12	12	8	6

For a more detailed approach to budgeting your time, complete steps 3–6. Otherwise, move ahead to step 7 and plan your calendar (p. 152).

● *TIME BUDGET: Allocate your time by activity period in component 8 of your Referral Marketing Plan (appendix B).*

Step 3: Allocate Time per Source

Allocate part of the total available time to each source. In our example, we have 120 hours available for six sources this year. We can allocate 20 hours to each — or, more realistically, we can apportion it unevenly, depending on how important we consider each source:

Referral Source	Total Hours Available
No. 1	30
No. 2	20
No. 3	25
No. 4	15
No. 5	20
No. 6	10
Total	120

We recommend that you budget for no more than ten individuals the first time around. As you develop and refine your system, you can expand your network of referral sources.

Step 4: Determine the Number of Contacts per Source

Taking into consideration the total time you allocated to each referral source in step 3, decide how many times you wish to contact each source during the campaign. Classify each as a daily, weekly, monthly, quarterly, semiannual, or other target. Sources you contact less than twice a year cannot truly be considered primary referral sources.

Referral Source	Total Hours Available	Contacts per Campaign
No. 1	30	*24 (twice per month)*
No. 2	20	*12 (monthly)*
No. 3	25	*17 (every third week)*
No. 4	15	*12 (monthly)*
No. 5	20	*12 (monthly)*
No. 6	10	*6 (every other month)*
Total	120	

Step 5: Determine the Length of Each Contact

Distribute the time you assigned each target in step 3 among the contacts you identified in step 4. For example, you allocated 30 hours to source no. 1 for the 12-month period, and you will make 24 contacts. How much of the 30 hours should you allocate to each of the 24 contacts? It's unlikely that you would distribute the time evenly, with each meeting lasting an hour and a quarter. For simplicity, make 18 of the contacts 1 hour each, and give 2 hours to each of the other 6 contacts.

Referral Source	Total Hours Available	Contacts per Campaign
No. 1	30	*24 (18 @ 1.0h; 6 @ 2.0h)*
No. 2	20	*12 (8 @ 1.5h; 4 @ 2.0h)*
No. 3	25	*17 (9 @ 1.0h; 8 @ 2.0h)*
No. 4	15	*12 (9 @ 1.0h; 3 @ 2.0h)*
No. 5	20	*12 (8 @ 1.5h; 4 @ 2.0h)*
No. 6	10	*6 (4 @ 1.5h; 2 @ 2.0h)*
Total	120	

Scheduling Tactics

How many contacts should you make? How often should you make them? Here are several ways to answer these questions and speed the process of developing effective, rewarding relationships.

1. Spread out your contacts. Regardless of the level of your relationship, the more contacts you can make with a source, the better. Two short meetings are more beneficial than one long session. Each meeting becomes an opportunity to strengthen the relationship, to move it along, to enhance your visibility and recognition. Your targets will remember you better.

2. Schedule predictably. Stay in contact with your targets regularly and consistently; train them to expect to hear from you at certain times. This tactic builds positive expectancy. For example, if you usually contact one of your sources during the first week of every quarter, she will come to expect it and will budget time for you. If she doesn't hear from you, she may call to see if something is wrong.

3. Link new contact activities with established ones. Getting into new routines is not easy, but one of the fastest and surest ways to establish good habits is to link them with old habits. For instance, if you never seem to get around to drafting letters that need to be written to your sources, but you always manage to browse the Web before lunch, resolve to draft a letter while you're waiting for all those Web page graphics to download. This guarantees that you'll have time every day to draft letters.

4. Make each contact lead to the next. Before concluding a meeting or telephone conversation, schedule the date of your next contact. In written correspondence, close by stating the date your target should expect to hear from you again: "I'll send you a note within forty-five days." Having made the commitment, you're more likely to follow through. This practice establishes a chain of contacts, with each meeting leading to the next.

5. Assume responsibility for making contact. You can't control whether a source will contact you when you need help; you can control only what you do yourself. Take the initiative; stay in touch with your source.

6. Stick to your plan. As your RMC achieves success and you establish routines with your sources, some of them may begin taking the contact initiative. Don't let these contacts interfere with your contact schedule — that is, don't count contacts they initiate as fulfillment of the contacts you've scheduled. By keeping to your schedule, you can subtly condition your referral sources and keep your plan on track.

Step 6: Determine the Time per Activity

In implementing your RMC, you will use your time in any or all of six activities:

Activity	Description
1. Assessing	Researching and determining needs
2. Planning	Decision making, forecasting, budgeting, and scheduling
3. Preparing	Developing tools and resources, including training, needed to carry out your plan of action
4. Implementing	Actions needed to achieve your goals: meetings, presentations, telephone calls, letters
5. Evaluating	Tracking and evaluating results
6. Other	All other activities

The time you reserved in step 5 for each contact will be used performing one or more of these activities. For example, if you allocated two hours to make your first contact with source no. 1, you might assign 20 minutes to each of the six activities — 20 minutes for assessing, 20 minutes for planning, 20 minutes for preparing, and so on. It's more likely, however, that these activities will require different amounts of time. Your first contact might require 30 minutes of assessing, 45 minutes of planning, 15 minutes of preparing, and 30 minutes of implementing.

To allocate your time and schedule your contacts, you may find it helpful to use the Time Allocation Tool in appendix A-11 to record your calculations.

Step 7: Set Up Your Calendar

When you've finished budgeting your time in a manner that you consider practical and achievable, set a target date for each contact on your Referral Marketing Plan. Add all other primary relationship development and referral marketing activities to this calendar, including the activities detailed in the forecasting and evaluation chapters that follow.

● *CALENDAR: Turn to component 9 of your Referral Marketing Plan (appendix B) and record your plans in your calendar. See the example in appendix C.*

BUDGETING AND ALLOCATING YOUR COSTS

SYSTEMATIC RELATIONSHIP DEVELOPMENT and referral marketing also requires you to estimate the cost of your activities. The steps involved are similar to those in budgeting your time. The first two are enough for a good general approach to estimating your costs, and they are all that you need to do to complete the tenth component of your Referral Marketing Plan. If you prefer a more detailed approach, continue with steps 3–6.

Step 1: Estimate Total Funds Available

Because the amount of money you have available will limit your marketing activities, don't implement your RMC until you've budgeted your costs. First, do one of two things:

- determine how much you have to spend, then select tactics (from chapter 12) you can use within those limitations; or
- plot what you would like to do, then establish a budget that will cover your costs.

For our example, we will use the latter approach and plan a twelve-month campaign with $2,400 total funds available for six prospective referral sources.

In real life, you'll have to decide on a total budget based on experience. Start with an estimate — an educated guess. How much can you spare? How much do your Network members spend? How much will you need to accomplish the activities you planned in your Time Allocation Tool? How much did you spend last year on similar activities — seminars, networking associations, business lunches? Try to dedicate at least as much for your first Referral Marketing Campaign. By channeling the money toward a specific purpose — increasing your referral business — you'll be making it work a lot more effectively than before.

All that's required now is to allocate your money over the period of your RMC (step 2). However, if you complete steps 3–6, you'll get a better idea of whether the figure you chose is a good estimate. If it isn't, raise or lower it and run through the steps again, repeating the exercise until you have a budget that works.

153

Step 2: Estimate Total Funds Available per Period

Allocate the available funds, $2,400, by month. We'll distribute our funds the same way we distributed our time, weighted seasonally:

	Month											
	1	2	3	4	5	6	7	8	9	10	11	12
$	240	240	240	240	200	160	160	160	240	240	160	120

● **COST BUDGET: Allocate your available funds by activity period in component 10 of your Referral Marketing Plan (appendix B).**

For a more detailed approach to budgeting your expenses, complete the next four steps. Otherwise, move ahead to chapter 19, "Forecasting Sales from Referrals."

Step 3: Determine the Funding Amount per Source

Having reserved $2,400 for our six selected referral sources, we will now decide how much money we'll need for each source. We could allocate the money equally, but since we're going to spend more time with some sources than with others, we should probably allocate the money more or less proportionately.

Referral Source	Funds Available
No. 1	$600
No. 2	$400
No. 3	$500
No. 4	$300
No. 5	$400
No. 6	$200
Total	$2,400

Step 4: Determine the Number of Contacts per Source

If this step sounds familiar, it should. It's the same fourth step you used to budget your RMC time (page 150). Use the figures you've already decided on.

Step 5: Determine the Funding per Contact

How much will you spend on each contact? In our example, we allocated $500 to source no. 3. We're going to meet 17 times with this source — 9 one-hour contacts and 8 two-hour contacts (page 150). How do we divide the $500 among these 17 contacts? Here's one way:

Contact Length	Cost per Contact	x	No. of Contacts	=	Total
1 hour	*$20*		9		*$180*
2 hours	*$40*		8		*$320*
Totals			17		*$500*

Continue by deciding which contacts will be one-hour contacts and which will be two-hour contacts. For example, you might find it advantageous to start with a two-hour meeting to discuss your proposal at length with your source. If so, contact no. 1 with this source will show a distribution of $40 among expense categories on your Cost Allocation Tool — that is, the bottom line will be $40 (appendix A-12).

Step 6: Determine Funding per Expense Category

Implementing your RMC will involve a variety of expenses. We've identified fourteen expense categories that will apply to most RMCs; you can add or delete categories to fit your circumstances.

Using the Cost Allocation Tool (appendix A-12), allocate the money you set aside for each contact (step 5) among these expense categories.

Expense Categories

1. Contributions/gifts/donations/sponsorships
2. Copying/printing/developing & processing
3. Entertainment
4. Facilities rental
5. Meals
6. Membership fees
7. Postage
8. Subscriptions
9. Self-development
10. Service fees/professional/consulting
11. Supplies & equipment
12. Telephone/fax/electronic mail
13. Travel (mileage, hotel, parking, taxi, etc.)
14. Other

Chapter 19

Forecasting Sales from Referrals

*Watching
the Road
Ahead*

BY THIS POINT you should have a pretty good idea of the shape and composition of your business and your Network, how you are going to use your Network, and how much time and money your Referral Marketing Campaign will cost you. The next step is to look down the road a bit and set goals. To set realistic goals, however, you must first answer the following questions: How do you expect your business to change as a result of your RMC? How many referrals do you expect to get? What dollar value do you expect to realize from these referrals? How many referral sources will you need to achieve these projections?

You could guess at the answers to these questions, but there's a better way — a systematic method of setting your goals using your experience as a base. First, look back at a recent period of sales revenues from referrals and all other sources (your reference period). Then project what you expect revenue to be as a result of your RMC (your first forecast). Your forecast should be based on four factors:

- the number of referrals you expect to receive;
- the dollar value of the referrals you expect to get;
- the percentage of your business you expect to result from referrals; and
- the number of sources you will need to achieve the expected number and dollar value of referrals.

ANALYZING YOUR REFERENCE PERIOD

THE FIRST THING you need to do is to analyze these four factors during a recent business period — your reference period. (Use the Reference Period Questions tool in appendix A-13). One year is usually the standard; if you've been in business less than a year or do not have twelve months of data to analyze, you may use a shorter period of time, such as nine, six, or three months.

Define Your Reference Period

First, set an end date and a start date for your reference period. For the end of the reference period, use the last day of the most recently completed month or the last day of your company's regular performance evaluation period or budget year.

If you set the end of the period as March 31 and specify an analysis period of twelve months, then April 1 of the prior year is the start date of the reference period (and April 1 of this year begins the new period that you will use for your first forecast).

Record Reference Period Information

Once you've specified your reference period, answer the following ten questions about your activities during that period. If this is your first time using systematic referral marketing, you probably can't answer all these questions. You will be able to, however, after you've completed your first new period.

Reference Period Questions

Start date: *April 1, 1997*   End date: *March 31, 1998*

Prospects

1. How many prospects did you generate or identify from all sources?	50
2. How many of these prospects were referred to you?	30
What percentage of all prospects does this represent?	60 %

Clients

3. How many new clients did you get from all sources?	15
4. How many of these new clients came from referrals?	10
What percentage of all new clients does this represent?	67 %

Sales

5. What was your sales total during the reference period?	$ 150K
6. How much of this was generated from referrals?	$ 90K
What percentage of all sales does this represent?	60 %

Referral Sources

7. How many sources provided the referred prospects identified in question 2?	20
8. What was the average number of referred prospects per source?	2.5
9. How many sources provided you with the new referred clients identified in question 4?	6
10. What was the average number of referred clients per source?	2.5

The answers to these questions will establish a baseline against which you will measure your first forecast. A year from now (or after whatever period you specify), you can compare the results you realize from your RMC with the projections you are about to make.

YOUR FIRST FORECAST

THE NEXT STEP is to write down what you expect to achieve during a future period. Your reference period determines your first forecast period. If your reference period is the year ending March 31, 1998, your forecast period is April 1, 1998–March 31, 1999.

To make your projections, you simply answer the same questions, slightly revised, by plugging in the appropriate data for the forecast period (First Period Projections, appendix A-14), then comparing your answers with the reference period. For example, you know that 30 prospects came to you by referral in the reference period (question 2 above), and you expect to get 45 new prospects by referral in your forecast period (question 2 below). This is a 50 percent increase (15 ÷ 30 = .50).

Your projections of total sales from this worksheet become part of your Referral Marketing Plan. In our example, we expect total sales to be $200,000 (question no. 5 below), of which $150,000 — that is, 75 percent — will be from referrals (question no. 6).

Sales Projections

Product/service	Unit price	No. units expected to be sold	Total projected sales	Expected sales from referrals	Expected % sales from referrals
Executive Coaching	$200/h	500	$100,000	$70,000	70%
CFO for Rent®	$5,000/mo	10	$50,000	$35,000	70%
Exec. Search	$2,000	10	$20,000	$20,000	100%
Exec. Seminars	$3,000	10	$30,000	$25,000	83%

Tot. sales exp. during campaign period: A. **$200,000** B. **$150,000**

Expected % of total sales from referrals: C. **75** %

● **SALES AND REFERRAL PROJECTIONS: To complete component 11 of your Referral Marketing Plan (appendix B), enter your answers to question 5 in blank A and question 6 in blanks B and C.**

In answering question no. 7 on your first period projection, assume that the number of referrals generated by each source during period 1 will be the same as during the reference period. For example, if you averaged 5 referred prospects per source during the reference period, then you would need 100 sources (500 divided by 5) to get 500 referred prospects, or 1,400 (7,000 divided by 5) for 7,000 referred prospects.

First Period Projections

Start date: **April 1, 1998**   End date: **March 31, 1999**

Prospects

1. How many prospects do you expect to generate from all sources? | **60**

   Forecast no. 1: The number of prospects generated will (increase/decrease) by **+20%** compared with the reference period.

2. How many of the prospects you generate do you expect to result from referrals? | **45**

   What percentage of all prospects will this represent? | **75** %

   Forecast no. 2: The percentage of prospects generated from referrals will (increase/decrease) by | **+50%**

Clients

3. How many new clients do you expect to generate from all sources? | **20**

   Forecast no. 3: The number of clients generated will (increase/decrease) by **+33%** compared with the reference period.

4. How many clients do you expect to generate from the referred prospects? | **15**

   What percentage of all new clients will this represent? | **75** %

   Forecast no. 4: The percentage of clients generated from referrals will (increase/decrease) by | **+50%**

Sales

5. How much do you expect to generate in sales? | **$200K**

   Forecast no. 5: Total sales will (increase/decrease) by **+33%** compared with the reference period.

6. How much of the total sales do you expect to result from referred clients? | **$150K**

   What percentage of total sales will this represent? | **75** %

   Forecast no. 6: Sales resulting from referrals will (increase/decrease) by **$+60K**, and the percentage of total sales resulting from referrals will (increase/decrease) by | **+15%**

Referral Sources

7. How many sources do you expect you will need to generate the expected number of referred prospects? | **30**

   Forecast no. 7: The number of sources needed to generate the expected referred prospects will (increase/decrease) by | **+50%**

8. What will be the average number of referred prospects per source? (Enter the reference period average.) | **2.5**

9. How many sources do you expect will be needed to generate the number of referred clients you expect (using the average from reference period question 10)? | **6**

10. What will be the average number of referred clients per source? (Enter the reference period average.) | **2.5**

BEYOND PERIOD 1

AFTER YOU HAVE COMPLETED one period of your RMC and compared the results with the projections based on your reference period, you'll be ready to adjust your RMC and set up new projections. Close scrutiny of how your results diverged from your expectations should help you forecast future results more accurately.

To forecast your referrals and sales for period 2 and beyond, simply make the previous period your new reference period, then answer the questions as you did for your period 1 forecast. For periods beyond your first projection, note that we have added several questions (Projections Beyond First Period, appendix A-15).

This first step in determining desired outcome — projecting what you expect to achieve by the end of each period — gives your RMC focus and direction. It also establishes several of the yardsticks that you will be using to evaluate its success.

Chapter 20

Tracking and Evaluating Results

Monitoring and Adjusting Your Plan

F OR AN INDIVIDUAL BUSINESSPERSON, as well as for an organization, an essential part of any marketing plan is measuring the results. Your Referral Marketing Campaign is no exception. To use your sources wisely and efficiently, you've got to know whether and how well your RMC is working, how you can change it to improve current and future results, and how much your investment of time and money is earning you.

There are ways to track and evaluate your progress. You must first decide, of course, what to evaluate. In general, you will need to track several kinds of data:

- activities by sources named in your RMC that produced information, support, or referrals, even if no business resulted;
- activities by other sources that produced information, support, or referrals, even if no business resulted; and
- the amount of time and money you spent on your RMC.

TRACKING AND EVALUATION TOOLS

WE'VE DESIGNED THREE TOOLS you can use to track and evaluate your referral marketing activities. Below are examples showing how each tool is used; you can use the blank forms in appendices A-16, A-17, and A-18 to evaluate the results of your own RMC. Don't limit yourself to what you find here. A little independent research will uncover many other useful tools — simple and complex, short term and long term, manual and automatic, free and for sale — for monitoring and evaluating your progress and results.

Tracking Tool 1: Contact Report

Your main tool for recording the data you need to evaluate your RMC's effectiveness is the Contact Report (appendix A-16). On this report you detail the activities leading to and the results of contacts, both planned and unplanned, with a specific source. After each meaningful interaction, document the purpose of the contact, the topics you discussed, the benefits and their estimated value for both the source and yourself, your expenses, the time you spent, any actions you need to take, and ideas for improving your next contact or other aspects of your RMC.

Contact Report

Use this tool to document the results of planned and unplanned contacts with a referral source. Fill it out as soon as possible after your contact, and answer each question as fully as possible.

Person contacted ___John Kinde___ [X] planned [ ] unplanned

Type of contact [X] face to face [ ] correspondence [ ] phone [ ] other

Contact date _4/1/98_ time _10 am_ location _My office in LA_

1. What were the circumstances that led to this contact (name of event, how introduced, etc.)?
   John wanted my feedback on some research he plans to conduct

2. What were your goals for this contact?
   A. Give John with the feedback he needs
   B. Provide info about my future plans to get more referral business

3. What topics were covered or discussed?
   A. Hotel industry survey B. Draft of promotional materials
   C. Target list

4. What relationship development and referral marketing tactics did you use?
   A. Advising B. Collaborating

5. What actions did your source agree to take? When?
   Liked idea of helping each other generate referrals.
   No action required at this time.

6. What actions did you agree to take? When?
   Follow up with more details by early June

7. What did you gain from this contact? (Approx. value: $_____)
   More knowledge about his target market

8. What did your source gain as a result of this contact? (Approx. value: $_____)
   Candid feedback on survey format

9. About how much time did the contact take, including preparation? _1_ hours _30_ minutes
   If contact was planned, what accounts for the difference between expected and actual time spent?
   45 minutes extra to accommodate John's desire for feedback

10. Itemize all expenses incurred and calculate the total cost.

Expense description	Amount
Refreshments	*$3.50*

    If this was a planned contact, what accounts for the difference between expected and actual costs?
    Less was spent because we did not go out for breakfast

11. If this was a planned contact, how would you rate the overall results?
    [ ] Exceeded anticipated results [X] Met anticipated results [ ] Fell short of anticipated results

12. What could have been done to produce better results?
    Nothing

Business Referral Tool

Report no. _____5_____ Date received _9/15/98_

Section 1: Referral Source

Name ___Joan Irvine___ Title ___Nurse___

Company _____Kaiser Hospital_____

Business address ___10800 Magnolia Ave., Riverside, CA___

Home address ___706 N. Broadacres, Compton, CA 90220___

Bus. phone _(909) 555-2662_ Home phone _(310) 555-1032_ Fax _N/A_

Web page ___N/A___ E-mail ___N/A___

Referral source profile data:

        Nurse of the Month

Section 2: Prospect

Name ___John Haskell___ Title _President_

Company _Cori Management Group_

Address _1035 Alta Vista Ave., Munster, IN 46321_

Phone ___(219) 555-3666___

Best time to reach _Early morning_

Prospect profile data: Decision maker? [X] Yes [ ] No

Relationship between referral source and prospect:

  College classmate

Relationship between referral source and prospect's organization:

  None

Section 3: Reason for the Referral

What does the prospect's organization need? How do I know this?

  Executive coaching — not sure

What is being done now to meet this need?

  Unknown

How is it working?

How will I be able to help or work with this group?

What triggered the referral?

  Referral source spoke at class reunion

Section 4: Organization's profile data

Primary mission:
Unknown

Products or services:
Provides facilities management services

Company history:
Unknown

Locations:
Indiana, California, New York

Number of employees:
50

Key contacts:
John Haskell

Section 5: Referral development plan and activities Date: _____

Actions taken by me, prospect, referral source:
Referral source to get more information about company within next 90 days

Results:

Current/final status:

Section 6: Quality of support or referral

Appropriateness of referral:

| Inappropriate — not what I do | | | | | | Very appropriate — it's me | | | |
| 1 | 2 | 3 | 4 | 5 | 6 | 7 | 8 | 9 | 10 |

Readiness to buy:

| Cold | | | | | | | | Extremely hot | |
| 1 | 2 | 3 | 4 | 5 | 6 | 7 | 8 | 9 | 10 |

Prospect's decision-making power:

| None | | | | | | | Complete control | | |
| 1 | 2 | 3 | 4 | 5 | 6 | 7 | 8 | 9 | 10 |

Source's influence:

| None | | | | | | | | Extensive | |
| 1 | 2 | 3 | 4 | 5 | 6 | 7 | 8 | 9 | 10 |

Quality of help provided by the source:

| Poor | | | | | | | | Significant | |
| 1 | 2 | 3 | 4 | 5 | 6 | 7 | 8 | 9 | 10 |

When I made initial contact, what did the prospect know about me?

Dollar value of the referral:

| ☐ | ☐ | ☐ | ☐ | ☐ |
| $0 | | $50,000 | | $100,000 or more |

Event Report

Use this form to document the results of your participation in various referral marketing events such as conferences, mixers, dinner parties, fund-raisers, seminars, and programs. Attach documents such as agendas, programs, participant lists, and handouts to the report when available.

Type of event: *Seminar* Date: *5/3/97* from *9:30 am* to *3:30 pm*

Brief description: Location: *Hypmovation Bldg.* Parking: *Free*
  101 W. Alameda Ave.
  Burbank, CA 91502

Sponsors: *Allstar Alliance* Contact info: *Jeannie Esposito, (800) 817-8278*

Event coordinators: *Same* Contact info: *Same*

Approx. no. of attendees: *15* Total no. of people met: *15*

No. of new contacts made: *9* No. of recontacts made: *6*

List of attachments:

☐ attendance roster ☐ copy of business cards ☐ seating chart

☐ introduction worksheet ☐ event evaluation ☐ program

☐ pictures taken ☐ miscellaneous ☒ other: *Promotional flyer*

See the following individuals or organizations for additional information:

Benefits received/estimated value/source/contact information:

A. Upcoming events/opportunities discovered:

B. New ideas/suggestions: *Got an idea on how to structure my next demo video*

C. Materials collected: *(1) Complimentary tape from Jim Cathcart on how to work with meeting planners*

(2) 110-page workbook

D. New knowledge/skills: *Insights into the needs of meeting planners*

E. Discounted purchases:

F. Gifts, prizes, complimentary meals, tickets, etc.:

G. Recognition, awards, exposure: *Instructor promoted my book; had it on display*

H. Key contacts/introductions: *Was able to strengthen relationships with 6 of my colleagues; discovered more about each other*

I. Other: *Sold 2 books as a result of attending this seminar*

Overall assessment: Rate event in each area shown below using this scale:
1. excellent   2. very good   3. good   4. fair   5. poor

	Rating	Comments, contact information
Speaker:	1	*Jeannie Esposito. Topic: Get Ready, Provided practical information; (818) 555-2298*
Food:	1	*Complimentary pastry*
Service:		
Facilities:	3	*Not much space — had to hold notes in hand*
Parking:	3	*Limited space — several participants parked on street*
Sports:	1	
Entertainment:	N/A	
Organization:	2	
Handouts:	1	*Excellent notebook*
Attendance:	1	
Cost:	2	*$90*
Overall:	1	

Recommendations:

Investments made/people you helped:

Name	Address/phone	Type of assistance provided
Maria Lopez		*Several ideas on how to select topics*
Marianne Mathis		*Provided two contacts*

Approximately how much time was spent on this event (including planning, preparation, traveling, etc.)? _____days _10_ hours

Itemize all expenses incurred in connection with this event and calculate the total:

Expense description	Amount
Registration	*$90*
Lunch	*10*
Travel (200 mi @ .31/mile)	*62*
	$162

Actions required:

People to contact:	Date due	Date completed
Jim Cathcart	*5/30*	
Marianne Mathis	*5/15*	*5/14*

Things to do:		
Send Bill Brooks a thank-you letter for event info	*5/4*	*5/4*

Send copies of report to:		
Grace Breur	*5/4*	*5/6*
Steve Stewart	*5/4*	*5/6*

Tracking Tool 2: Business Referral Tool

Each time you receive a referral, fill out a Business Referral Tool (appendix A-17). As a reminder, this report has six sections in which you record information about

- the source of the referral;
- your prospect;
- the circumstances leading to the referral;
- the business organization;
- your plans, activities, and results, including purchases; and
- the quality of the support or referral.

You should update each Business Referral Tool as needed over the course of your RMC.

Tracking Tool 3: Event Report

The Event Report (appendix A-18) documents the results of your participation in various referral marketing events, such as conferences, seminars, programs, mixers, dinner parties, and fund-raisers. On this report you record, among other information,

- sponsors,
- the number of people attending,
- specific benefits received, and
- recommendations.

Whenever possible or appropriate, attach a program agenda, a list of participants, and any handouts you can obtain.

If you work for someone else, there are several ways you can use the Event Report. Share it with your manager and other members of the department who could not attend. Your management is more likely to give you the time off to go to these events if you can report on their actions and their value — not just the value for you, but for the whole organization.

KNOWING WHERE YOU'RE GOING

I T'S IMPORTANT TO KEEP TRACK of your results and to be as up to date as you can on how well your Referral Marketing Campaign is working. You may feel, at first, that these tools take up too much of your valuable time. That's understandable; none of us enjoy all the paperwork it takes to maintain a business, especially information-reporting forms that seem to get sent off into

● *TRACKING AND EVALUATION: Summarize the activities and results of your RMC in component 12 of your Referral Marketing Plan (appendix B),*

limbo or stored away and forgotten. But if you get into the habit of keeping track of this information, and if you stay alert for and respond to changes, you'll find using these tools gets easier — and your increased business efficiency will more than make up for the time you spend.

Try these tools for a while; if they don't fit, adapt them to suit your purposes. There are many different ways to track and evaluate the results of your referral marketing activities. Besides the logs, questionnaires, checklists, and profiles presented in this book, you can use computer software programs. Two that we often recommend are ACT and Goldmine.

With a thorough tracking and evaluation system, you'll know whether your plan is working and whether it's cost effective. You'll be able to demonstrate to managers, investors, bankers, and employees that you're a focused and capable marketing professional. Be patient, persistent, flexible, and imaginative, and you'll eventually find yourself running a successful referral-based business, one that will be the envy of other businesses.

Part

VII

Tools

Appendix A

Relationship Development and Referral Marketing Tools

1. Product/Service Description Tool (chapter 4)
2. Target Market Description Tool (chapter 4)
3. Identifying Specific Targets (chapter 4)
4. Information Network Component Tool (chapter 7)
5. Support Network Component Tool (chapter 8)
6. Referral Network Component Tool (chapter 9)
7. Universal Business Network Tool (chapter 10)
8. Business Network Voids Tool (chapter 10)
9. GAINS Profile (chapter 11)
10. Quiz: Facts You Should Know about Each Member of Your Network (chapter 11)
11. Time Allocation Tool (chapter 18)
12. Cost Allocation Tool (chapter 18)
13. Reference Period Questions (chapter 19)
14. First Period Projections (chapter 19)
15. Projections Beyond First Period (chapter 19)
16. Contact Report (chapter 20)
17. Business Referral Tool (chapter 20)
18. Event Report (chapter 20)

Product/Service Description Tool

Write the name of one product or service you will market by referral:

_____

Answer each of the following questions about the product or service named.
Describe the product or service (size, shape, color, activities, etc.).

_____
_____
_____
_____

What are the key features of the product or service?

_____
_____
_____
_____

What is the purpose of this product or service?

_____
_____
_____
_____

What needs does this product or service satisfy for users?

_____
_____
_____
_____

How is your product or service delivered?

_____
_____
_____
_____

How much does your product or service cost (including volume discounts,
payment terms, incentives)? _____

_____
_____
_____
_____

Target Market Description Tool

For the product or service you described in the Product/Service Description Tool (appendix A-1), answer the following questions (write N/A if the question does not apply to your target market).

Name of product or service: _____

I. What geographic market(s) do you concentrate on?

Now   Desired

A. Worldwide/international markets (list up to 3 countries)

1._____   1._____
2._____   2._____
3._____   3._____

B. U.S. markets (list up to 3 states)

1._____   1._____
2._____   2._____
3._____   3._____

C. State markets (list up to 3 cities or counties in one of the states in B)

1._____   1._____
2._____   2._____
3._____   3._____

D. City/county markets (list up to 3 local communities in one of the cities in C)

1._____   1._____
2._____   2._____
3._____   3._____

II. What major market segment does your target market represent?

☐ Consumers   ☐ Organizations/businesses   ☐ Both

(Complete section II if you target organizations or businesses.)

Now   Desired

A. What industries do you target for your product or service (e.g., health care, financial services, entertainment)?

1._____   1._____
2._____   2._____
3._____   3._____

B. Within one of the industries selected in A, what companies do you target for your product or services (e.g., Citibank, First Interstate, Wells Fargo in the financial services industry)?

1._____   1._____
2._____   2._____
3._____   3._____

C. Within one of the companies selected in B, what divisions, departments, or sections do you target (e.g., human resources, marketing, purchasing)?

1._____   1._____

2._____   2._____

3._____   3._____

D. Within one of the divisions, departments, or sections you selected in C, what are the occupation titles of the individuals you attempt to contact (e.g., trainer, recruiter, administrator in human services)?

1._____   1._____

2._____   2._____

3._____   3._____

III. What are the demographics and psychographics of your desired target market? (Complete this section if you target consumers.)

Describe your typical customer. Provide your own categories for each area if the breakdown outlined is inappropriate.

A. Age group (you may use numerical breakdown, e.g., 20–30 years):

☐ Infants   ☐ Children   ☐ Teenagers   ☐ Adults   ☐ Senior citizens

B. Sex: ☐ Male   ☐ Female   ☐ Both

C. Marital status: ☐ Married   ☐ Single   ☐ Both

D. Family size:

☐ No children   ☐ 1–2 children   ☐ 3–5   ☐ 6–9   ☐ 10 or more

E. Annual family income/average earnings:

☐ Under $10K ☐ $10–30K ☐ $30–50K ☐ $50–70K ☐ $70–90K ☐ Over $90K

F. Ethnic group/nationality:

☐ African American   ☐ Hispanic American   ☐ Asian American   ☐ Other

G. Education:

☐ Grade school   ☐ High school   ☐ College   ☐ Graduate school

H. Buying patterns:

I. Other considerations (e.g., physical features, height, weight, religious affiliation, political views, family orientation, occupation, lifestyle, attitude, values, beliefs):

1._____

2._____

3._____

Identifying Specific Targets

In referral marketing, each target market represents a specific individual. Write the names of 5 individuals, either current or prospective clients, to whom you want to market each product or service for which you completed a Product/ Service Description Tool.

Product or service: _____

Name, address, phone no.

1. _____
2. _____
3. _____
4. _____
5. _____

Product or service: _____

Name, address, phone no.

1. _____
2. _____
3. _____
4. _____
5. _____

Product or service: _____

Name, address, phone no.

1. _____
2. _____
3. _____
4. _____
5. _____

Product or service: _____

Name, address, phone no.

1. _____
2. _____
3. _____
4. _____
5. _____

Information Network Component Tool

1. People who are trying to achieve the same things you want to achieve:

Name	Address	Phone

   1. _____

   2. _____

   3. _____

2. People who are in the business or profession you are in or want to enter:

   1. _____

   2. _____

   3. _____

3. People who were in the business or profession you are in or want to enter:

   1. _____

   2. _____

   3. _____

4. People who write or produce books, tapes, or videos in your industry or specialty:

   1. _____

   2. _____

   3. _____

5. People who regulate, audit, or monitor others in your field:

   1. _____

   2. _____

   3. _____

6. People who train others in your profession:

   1. _____

   2. _____

   3. _____

7. People who advise or consult with people in your field:

   1. _____

   2. _____

   3. _____

8. Members of trade, business, or professional organizations in your field:

   1. _____

   2. _____

   3. _____

Support Network Component Tool

1. Your mentors, current or past:

   Name   Address   Phone

   1. _____
   2. _____
   3. _____

2. People you have taught or mentored:

   1. _____
   2. _____
   3. _____

3. People you have helped:

   1. _____
   2. _____
   3. _____

4. Your co-workers, colleagues, associates, and classmates:

   1. _____
   2. _____
   3. _____

5. Your family and close friends:

   1. _____
   2. _____
   3. _____

6. Other members of nonbusiness groups:

   1. _____
   2. _____
   3. _____

7. Your former managers, supervisors, and instructors:

   1. _____
   2. _____
   3. _____

8. Your church leaders, members, and groups:

   1. _____
   2. _____
   3. _____

Referral Network Component Tool

1. People in your contact sphere:

     Name   Address   Phone

    1. _____

    2. _____

    3. _____

2. Current or former clients:

    1. _____

    2. _____

    3. _____

3. People who get more business when you get more business:

    1. _____

    2. _____

    3. _____

4. People you do business with, other than your suppliers and vendors:

    1. _____

    2. _____

    3. _____

5. Current or former staff members, part time or full time:

    1. _____

    2. _____

    3. _____

6. People you have given referrals to:

    1. _____

    2. _____

    3. _____

7. Anyone who has given you referrals:

    1. _____

    2. _____

    3. _____

8. Other members of business referral groups:

    1. _____

    2. _____

    3. _____

Universal Business Network Tool

Listed below are several classifications of occupations. The categories represent occupations that, as an entrepreneur, you may need in the future. Write down at least one person who has expertise in or an affiliation with each of the categories. Space is provided for you to add other occupations relevant to your business.

Occupation	Name	Address	Phone

Accountant _____

Attorney _____

Banker _____

Business consultant _____

Chamber of
  Commerce officer _____

City business license/
  tax authority _____

Cleaning/maintenance
  service person _____

College/university
  administrator/staff _____

Commercial
  property broker _____

Computer consultant _____

Contractor _____

Credit card service
  representative _____

Credit check/
  collection agent _____

Electrician _____

Entertainment agent _____

Fund-raiser _____

Gardener _____

Handyperson _____

Hotel manager/
  key staff member _____

Human resources/
   personnel professional _____

Insurance
   agent/broker _____

Internal Revenue
   Service staff member _____

Librarian _____

Lobbyist _____

Minority/woman-owned
   business development
   center representative _____

Office supply/
   equipment
   service person _____

Personal agent _____

Photographer _____

Physician/nurse _____

Political official _____

Printer _____

Regional planning
   committee member _____

Restaurant
   manager/caterer _____

Secretarial service
   owner/employee _____

Security guard _____

SCORE counselor _____

SBA staff member/
   representative _____

Travel agent _____

Visitors and convention
   bureau official _____

Writer _____

Others _____

Business Network Voids Tool

List the Network component categories in which you could not think of as many as three sources. Each blank indicates a void in your Network. These are the professions and specialties in which you should try to develop a source.

Information Network voids

1. _____
2. _____
3. _____
4. _____
5. _____
6. _____
7. _____
8. _____

Support Network voids

1. _____
2. _____
3. _____
4. _____
5. _____
6. _____
7. _____
8. _____

Referral Network voids

1. _____
2. _____
3. _____
4. _____
5. _____
6. _____
7. _____
8. _____

Universal Business Network voids

1. _____
2. _____
3. _____
4. _____
5. _____
6. _____
7. _____
8. _____
9. _____
10. _____
11. _____
12. _____
13. _____
14. _____
15. _____
16. _____
17. _____
18. _____
19. _____
20. _____
21. _____
22. _____
23. _____
24. _____
25. _____
26. _____

GAINS Profile

Use this form to record goals, accomplishments, interests, networks, and skills —
your own, or those of your Network members or others with whom you want to
build a relationship. Use one form per individual; attach sheets as necessary.
Date each entry so you will know how old the information is. Use the other side
of this form to record information that doesn't fit one of the categories listed.

Name _____ Date _____

Goals _____

_____

_____

_____

_____

Accomplishments _____

_____

_____

_____

_____

Interests _____

_____

_____

_____

_____

Networks _____

_____

_____

_____

_____

Skills _____

_____

_____

_____

_____

Quiz: Facts You Should Know about Each Member of Your Network

Select a Network member with whom you are familiar and supply the following information about him or her. Try to complete the quiz within 15 minutes without help. Use your memory and any personal or professional resources at your disposal, such as directories, card files, notes, and online data. If the correct response is "none" or "not applicable," write "none." If you don't know the answer, leave it blank. Score 4 points for each complete, correct answer; 2 points for each partial answer. Highest possible score: 100 points. This exercise is most valuable if you discuss the answers with the individual after you finish.

Name _____

Personal information: **Points**

A. Nickname _____ ☐

B. Date and place of birth _____ ☐

C. A favorite color or food _____ ☐

D. Best friend (other than yourself) _____ ☐

E. Mentor/sponsor/role model/hero (other than yourself) _____
   _____ ☐

F. Favorite TV program, song, or hobby _____ ☐

G. A personal award or recognition _____ ☐

H. Type of pet or vehicle _____ ☐

Answer either the Employment or the Business/enterprise section below.

Employment:

I. Name and location of current place of employment _____
   _____ ☐

J. Job title and at least one major duty _____ ☐

K. Name and title of current boss _____ ☐

L. Name of one co-worker _____ ☐

M. A work-related award or achievement _____ ☐

N. Career objective or plan _____
   _____ ☐

O. Name and location of another company he or she has worked for
   _____ ☐

Business/enterprise:

I. Name and location of business _____ ☐

J. Name, key benefits, features, and price of one product or service

_____ ☐

K. One type of individual or group in target market _____ ☐

L. Major business issue/objective/problem _____

_____ ☐

M. Reason he or she decided to enter this business _____

_____ ☐

N. Number of years in this business or industry _____ ☐

O. Name of a vendor, staff member, or client _____

_____ ☐

Memberships:

P. One or more of the community groups, clubs, or organizations
he or she has belonged to, office or position held, and name of
at least one other member _____

_____ ☐

Q. One or more of the business associations or groups he or she
has belonged to, office or position held, and name of at least
one other member _____

_____ ☐

Residence and family:

R. City of residence _____ ☐

S. Home phone number _____ ☐

T. Name, occupation of spouse/significant other _____ ☐

U. No. children or siblings (and at least one name) _____ ☐

V. A parent's or guardian's name and occupation _____

_____ ☐

Education:

W. Name of at least one school attended (high school, college,
vocational, etc.) _____ ☐

X. Certificate, degree, credentials, license, or special training
received _____ ☐

Y. Newspaper, magazine, newsletter, or other publication
read regularly for educational or information about events
and opportunities _____ ☐

Total points ☐

Time Allocation Tool

Use this worksheet to calculate and record how your time will be allocated to each referral source, contact, and activity.

Referral marketing period: Start date _____ End date _____

Step 1: Write down the total time you plan to reserve for your RMC: _____ hrs per mo/yr/other

Step 2: Overall time allocation
Period: ☐ week ☐ month ☐ other

1	2	3	4	5	6	7	8	9	10	11	12
__	__	__	__	__	__	__	__	__	__	__	__

Step 3: Fill in the names of your referral sources and the time you plan to allocate to each. Remember, the sum of the times you assign to all your targets must equal the total number of hours available that you projected in step 1.

Referral source   Allocated time

1. _____   _____

2. _____   _____

3. _____   _____

4. _____   _____

5. _____   _____

6. _____   _____

                                   Total time allocated   _____

Steps 4, 5, and 6: Initially, estimate for each contact how much time you will need for each activity (see step 6, page 152). Keep track of the actual time you spend. Later, adjust these guidelines to reflect your needs.

Referral source no. _____ (use one or more sheets per target)

Activity	Contact number 1	2	3	4	5	6	7	8	Total time per activity
1. Assessing	__	__	__	__	__	__	__	__	_____
2. Planning	__	__	__	__	__	__	__	__	_____
3. Preparing	__	__	__	__	__	__	__	__	_____
4. Implementing	__	__	__	__	__	__	__	__	_____
5. Evaluating	__	__	__	__	__	__	__	__	_____
6. Other	__	__	__	__	__	__	__	__	_____
Total time per contact (from step 5)	__	__	__	__	__	__	__	__	

                    Total time allocated to source (from step 3) _____

Step 7: Set a target date for each contact on your Referral Marketing Plan calendar.

Cost Allocation Tool

Use this worksheet to calculate and record how your cost will be allocated to each referral source, contact, and expense category. Adapt worksheets as necessary.

Referral marketing period: Start date_____ End date _____

Step 1: Write down the total amount you plan to reserve for your RMC: $_____

Step 2: Overall cost allocation

Period: ☐ week ☐ month ☐ other

1	2	3	4	5	6	7	8	9	10	11	12
___	___	___	___	___	___	___	___	___	___	___	___

Step 3: Fill in the names of your referral sources and the dollar amount you plan to allocate to each. Remember, the sum of these amounts should equal the total you projected in step 1.

Referral source   Allocated cost

1. _____ $_____
2. _____   _____
3. _____   _____
4. _____   _____
5. _____   _____
6. _____   _____

Total amount budgeted $_____

Steps 4, 5, and 6: Initially, estimate for each contact how much money you will need for each expense category (see step 6, page 155). Keep track of the actual amount you spend. Later, adjust these guidelines to reflect your needs.

Referral source no. _____ (use one or more sheets per target)

Expense category	Contact number 1	2	3	4	5	6	7	8	Total cost per category
1. Contributions	$___	___	___	___	___	___	___	___	$_____
2. Copying/printing	___	___	___	___	___	___	___	___	_____
3. Entertainment	___	___	___	___	___	___	___	___	_____
4. Facilities rental	___	___	___	___	___	___	___	___	_____
5. Meals	___	___	___	___	___	___	___	___	_____
6. Membership fees	___	___	___	___	___	___	___	___	_____
7. Postage	___	___	___	___	___	___	___	___	_____
8. Subscriptions	___	___	___	___	___	___	___	___	_____
9. Self-development	___	___	___	___	___	___	___	___	_____
10. Service fees	___	___	___	___	___	___	___	___	_____
11. Supplies, equipment	___	___	___	___	___	___	___	___	_____
12. Phone/fax/e-mail	___	___	___	___	___	___	___	___	_____
13. Travel	___	___	___	___	___	___	___	___	_____
14. Other	___	___	___	___	___	___	___	___	_____
Total cost per contact (from step 3)	$___	___	___	___	___	___	___	___	

Total cost allocated to source (from step 3) $_____

Reference Period Questions

Start date: _____   End date: _____

Prospects

1. How many prospects did you generate or identify from all sources? [ ]

2. How many of these prospects were referred to you? [ ]

What percentage of all prospects does this represent? [%]

Clients

3. How many new clients did you get from all sources? [ ]

4. How many of these new clients came from referrals? [ ]

What percentage of all new clients does this represent? [%]

Sales

5. What was your sales total during the reference period? [$]

6. How much of this was generated from referrals? [$]

What percentage of all sales does this represent? [%]

Referral Sources

7. How many sources provided the referred prospects identified in question 2? [ ]

8. What was the average number of referred prospects per source? [ ]

9. How many sources provided you with the new referred clients identified in question 4? [ ]

10. What was the average number of referred clients per source? [ ]

First Period Projections

Start date: _____   End date: _____

Prospects

1. How many prospects do you expect to generate from all sources? [ ]

   Forecast no. 1: The number of prospects generated will (increase/decrease) by [%] compared with the reference period.

2. How many of the prospects you generate do you expect to result from referrals? [ ]

   What percentage of all prospects will this represent? [%]

   Forecast no. 2: The percentage of prospects generated from referrals will (increase/decrease) by [%]

Clients

3. How many new clients do you expect to generate from all sources? [ ]

   Forecast no. 3: The number of clients generated will (increase/decrease) by [%] compared with the reference period.

4. How many clients do you expect to generate from the referred prospects? [ ]

   What percentage of all new clients will this represent? [%]

   Forecast no. 4: The percentage of clients generated from referrals will (increase/decrease) by [%]

Sales

5. How much do you expect to generate in sales? [$]

   Forecast no. 5: Total sales will (increase/decrease) by [%] compared with the reference period.

6. How much of the total sales do you expect to result from referred clients? [$]

   What percentage of total sales will this represent? [%]

   Forecast no. 6: Sales resulting from referrals will (increase/decrease) by [$], and the percentage of total sales resulting from referrals will (increase/decrease) by [%]

Referral Sources

7. How many sources do you expect you will need to generate the expected number of referred prospects? [ ]

   Forecast no. 7: The number of sources needed to generate the expected referred prospects will (increase/decrease) by [%]

8. What will be the average number of referred prospects per source? (Enter the reference period average.) [ ]

9. How many sources do you expect will be needed to generate the number of referred clients you expect (using the average from reference period question 10)? [ ]

10. What will be the average number of referred clients per source? (Enter the reference period average.) [ ]

Projections Beyond First Period

Start date: _____   End date: _____

Prospects

1. How many prospects do you expect to generate from all sources? ☐

   Forecast no. 1: The number of prospects generated will (increase/decrease) by ☐ % compared with the reference period.

2. How many of the prospects you generate do you expect to result from referrals? ☐

   What percentage of all prospects will this represent? ☐ %

   Forecast no. 2: The percentage of prospects generated from referrals will (increase/decrease) by ☐ %

3. How many of the prospects generated do you expect to result from direct referrals (referrals you get from sources named in your RMC)? ☐

   Forecast no. 3: The number of prospects generated by direct referrals will constitute ☐ % of all new prospects.

Clients

4. How many new clients do you expect to generate from all sources? ☐

   Forecast no. 4: The number of clients generated will (increase/decrease) by ☐ % compared with the reference period.

5. How many clients do you expect to generate from referred prospects? ☐

   What percentage of all new clients will this represent? ☐ %

   Forecast no. 5: The number of clients generated from referrals will (increase/decrease) by ☐ %

6. How many clients do you expect to generate from prospects generated by direct referrals? ☐

   Forecast no. 6: The number of clients generated by direct referrals will amount to ☐ % of all new clients.

Sales

7. How much do you expect to generate in sales with your RMC during this period? $ ☐

   Forecast no. 7: Total sales will (increase/decrease) by ☐ % compared with the reference period.

8. How much of your total sales do you expect to result from referred clients?

   $ [   ]

   What percentage of total sales will this represent?

   [   ] %

   Forecast no. 8: Sales resulting from referrals will (increase/decrease) by $ [   ] , and the percentage of total sales resulting from referrals will (increase/decrease) by

   [   ] %

9. How much of your total sales do you expect to result from direct-referred clients?

   $ [   ]

   Forecast no. 9: Sales generated by clients resulting from direct referrals will constitute [   ] % of all sales.

Referral Sources

10. In the reference period, what was the average number of referred prospects per source?

    [   ]

    Based on this experience, how many sources will you need to generate the number of referred prospects you expect?

    [   ]

    Forecast no. 10: The number of sources needed to generate the expected level of referred prospects will (increase/decrease) by

    [   ] %

11. In the reference period, what was the average number of referred clients per source?

    [   ]

    Based on this experience, how many sources will you need to generate the number of referred clients you expect?

    [   ]

    Forecast no. 11: The number of sources needed to generate the expected level of referred clients will (increase/decrease) by

    [   ] %

12. In the reference period, what was the average number of direct-referred clients per source?

    [   ]

    Based on this experience, how many sources will you need to generate the number of direct-referred clients you expect?

    [   ]

    Forecast no. 12: The number of sources needed to generate the expected level of direct-referred clients will (increase/decrease) by

    [   ] %

Contact Report

Use this tool to document the results of planned and unplanned contacts with a referral source. Fill it out as soon as possible after your contact, and answer each question as fully as possible.

Person contacted _____ ☐ planned ☐ unplanned

Type of contact ☐ face to face ☐ correspondence ☐ phone ☐ other

Contact date _____ time _____ location _____

1. What were the circumstances that led to this contact (name of event, how introduced, etc.)?

2. What were your goals for this contact?

3. What topics were covered or discussed?

4. What relationship development and referral marketing tactics did you use?

5. What actions did your source agree to take? When?

6. What actions did you agree to take? When?

7. What did you gain from this contact?   (Approx. value: $ _____)

8. What did your source gain as a result of this contact? (Approx. value: $ _____)

9. About how much time did the contact take, including preparation?

_____ hours _____ minutes

If contact was planned, what accounts for the difference between expected and actual time spent?

10. Itemize all expenses incurred and calculate the total cost.

Expense description   Amount

If this was a planned contact, what accounts for the difference between expected and actual costs?

11. If this was a planned contact, how would you rate the overall results?

☐ Exceeded anticipated results

☐ Met anticipated results

☐ Fell short of anticipated results

12. What could have been done to produce better results?

Business Referral Tool

Report no. _____ Date received _____

Section 1: Referral Source

Name _____ Title _____

Company _____

Business address _____

Home address _____

Bus. phone _____ Home phone _____ Fax _____

Web page _____ E-mail _____

Referral source profile data:

Section 2: Prospect

Name _____ Title: _____

Company _____

Address _____

Phone _____

Best time to reach _____

Prospect profile data: Decision maker?   ☐ Yes   ☐ No

Relationship between referral source and prospect:

Relationship between referral source and prospect's organization:

Section 3: Reason for the Referral

What does the prospect's organization need? How do I know this?

What is being done now to meet this need?

How is it working?

How will I be able to help or work with this group?

What triggered the referral?

Section 4: Organization's profile data
Primary mission:

Products or services:

Company history:

Locations:

Number of employees:

Key contacts:

Section 5: Referral development plan and activities   Date: _____
Actions taken by me, prospect, referral source:

Results:

Current/final status:

Section 6: Quality of support or referral
Appropriateness of referral:
  Inappropriate — not what I do   Very appropriate — it's me
  1   2   3   4   5   6   7   8   9   10
Readiness to buy:
  Cold   Extremely hot
  1   2   3   4   5   6   7   8   9   10
Prospect's decision-making power:
  None   Complete control
  1   2   3   4   5   6   7   8   9   10
Source's influence:
  None   Extensive
  1   2   3   4   5   6   7   8   9   10
Quality of help provided by the source:
  Poor   Significant
  1   2   3   4   5   6   7   8   9   10
When I made initial contact, what did the prospect know about me?

Dollar value of the referral:
  ☐   ☐   ☐   ☐   ☐
  $0 $50,000 $100,000 or more

Event Report

Use this form to document the results of your participation in various referral marketing events such as conferences, mixers, dinner parties, fund-raisers, seminars, and programs. Attach documents such as agendas, programs, participant lists, and handouts to the report when available.

Type of event _____ Date _____ from _____ to _____

Brief description _____ Location _____ Parking _____

_____   _____ _____

Sponsors _____ Contact info _____

Event coordinators _____ Contact info _____

Approx. no. of attendees _____ Total no. of people met _____

No. of new contacts made _____ No. of recontacts made _____

List of attachments:

☐ attendance roster   ☐ copy of business cards   ☐ seating chart

☐ introduction worksheet   ☐ event evaluation   ☐ program

☐ pictures taken   ☐ miscellaneous   ☐ other _____

See the following individuals or organizations for additional information:

Benefits received/estimated value/source/contact information:

A. Upcoming events/opportunities discovered:

B. New ideas/suggestions:

C. Materials collected:

D. New knowledge/skills:

E. Discounted purchases:

F. Gifts, prizes, complimentary meals, tickets, etc.:

G. Recognition, awards, exposure:

H. Key contacts/introductions:

I. Other:

Overall assessment: Rate event in each area shown below using this scale:

1. excellent   2. very good   3. good   4. fair   5. poor

	Rating	Comments, contact information
Speaker	_____	_____
Food	_____	_____
Service	_____	_____
Facilities	_____	_____
Parking	_____	_____
Sports	_____	_____
Entertainment	_____	_____
Organization	_____	_____
Handouts	_____	_____
Attendance	_____	_____
Cost	_____	_____
Overall	_____	_____

Recommendations

Investments made/people you helped:

Name   Address/phone   Type of assistance provided

Approximately how much time was spent on this event (including planning, preparation, traveling, etc.)? _____ days _____ hours

Itemize all expenses incurred in connection with this event and calculate the total:

Expense description   Amount

Actions required   Date due   Date completed
  People to contact:

  Things to do:

  Send copies of report to:

Appendix B

Referral Marketing Plan

Component 1: Mission Statement

Component 2: Products and Services

Component 3: Target Market

Component 4: Competition

Component 5: Matching Needs and Prospective Sources

Component 6: Tactics

Component 7: Referral Marketing System

Component 8: Time Budget

Component 9: Calendar

Component 10: Cost Budget

Component 11: Sales and Referral Projections

Component 12: Tracking and Evaluation

Referral Marketing Plan
for

_____

Prepared by _____ Date prepared _____

Campaign start date _____ End date _____

Review the appropriate reference chapter indicated, then provide the
information indicated for each component of the plan.

Component 1: Mission Statement   Reference: Chapter 4

Write the mission statement for your business.

Component 2: Products and Services   Reference: Chapter 4

List the products and services you will use this marketing plan to promote. Briefly
describe each product or service.

Product/service   Description

Component 3: Target Market

Reference: Chapter 4

1. Market Description

Provide a general description of the primary market(s) you plan to target. Include demographic and psychographic information as appropriate.

2. Targeted Prospects

List the names of the specific individuals and (if names are not known) organizations you will target. List as many as you can effectively manage.

Name   Company

1._____   _____

2._____   _____

3._____   _____

4._____   _____

5._____   _____

6._____   _____

7._____   _____

Component 4: Competition

Reference: Chapter 4

1. Competitors

List and describe your primary competitors.

1._____

2._____

3._____

4._____

5._____

2. Unique Selling Position

How are you different from your primary competitors? Describe your unique competitive advantages.

Component 5: Matching Needs and Prospective Sources   Reference: Chapter 11

List the types of help you need and the prospective information, support, and referral source(s) that might provide this help

Type of help (#)	Description	Prospective source(s)
____	_____	_____
____	_____	_____
____	_____	_____
____	_____	_____
____	_____	_____
____	_____	_____
____	_____	_____
____	_____	_____
____	_____	_____
____	_____	_____
____	_____	_____
____	_____	_____

Component 6: Tactics   Reference: Chapter 12

List the primary relationship development and referral marketing tactics you plan to use during the campaign. Briefly describe how each will be used.

Tactic #	Tactic name	Description of use
____	_____	_____
____	_____	_____
____	_____	_____
____	_____	_____
____	_____	_____
____	_____	_____
____	_____	_____
____	_____	_____
____	_____	_____
____	_____	_____

Component 7: Referral Marketing System   Reference: Chapters 13, 14, 17

1. Key Sources

List the names of the key sources you will focus on during the campaign. List as many as you can manage effectively.

1._____
2._____
3._____
4._____
5._____
6._____
7._____
8._____
9._____
10._____

2. Briefing Your Sources

Describe the approaches you will use to brief your referral sources.

1._____
2._____
3._____
4._____
5._____
6._____

3. Rewarding and Recognizing Your Sources

Describe the methods you will use to recognize and reward your referral sources.

1._____
2._____
3._____
4._____
5._____

Component 8: Time Budget   Reference: Chapter 18

Distribute by period the total time available for your campaign.

Period: 1   2   3   4   5   6   7   8   9   10   11   12   Total

____ ____ ____ ____ ____ ____ ____ ____ ____ ____ ____ ____ ____

Component 9: Calendar   Reference: Chapter 18

List the major relationship development and referral marketing activities that will occur during your campaign.

Date   Activity

_____   _____

_____   _____

_____   _____

_____   _____

_____   _____

_____   _____

_____   _____

_____   _____

_____   _____

_____   _____

_____   _____

_____   _____

_____   _____

_____   _____

_____   _____

_____   _____

_____   _____

_____   _____

_____   _____

_____   _____

_____   _____

_____   _____

_____   _____

_____   _____

_____   _____

_____   _____

_____   _____

_____   _____

_____   _____

Component 10: Cost Budget   Reference: Chapter 18

Distribute by period the total funds available for your campaign.

Period: 1   2   3   4   5   6   7   8   9   10   11   12   Total

$ ___ ___ ___ ___ ___ ___ ___ ___ ___ ___ ___ ___ $___

Component 11: Sales and Referral Projections   Reference: Chapter 19

List the products and services you plan to sell during your campaign. Perform
the necessary calculations.

Product/ service	Unit price	No. units expected to be sold	Total projected sales	Expected sales from referrals	Expected % sales from referrals
1.					
2.					
3.					
4.					
5.					
6.					

Total sales expected during 1st period: A._____ B._____

Expected % of total sales from referrals: C._____

Component 12: Tracking and Evaluation   Reference: Chapter 20

List the tools and strategies that you will use to track, analyze, and evaluate the
results of your Referral Marketing Campaign. Include target dates for all actions.

APPENDIX C

REFERRAL MARKETING PLAN EXAMPLE

Referral Marketing Plan

for

Western Management Associates

Prepared by ___*Gene Siciliano*___ Date prepared *September 30, 1997*

Campaign start date ___*October 1, 1997*___ End date _September 30, 1998_

Review the appropriate reference chapter indicated, then provide the information indicated for each component of the plan.

Component 1: Mission Statement   Reference: Chapter 4

Write the mission statement for your business.

We are committed to helping business owners and corporate managers achieve greater financial success for their companies in an ever-changing economic environment by consulting on part-time financial management, business management coaching, executive search services, and management seminars and educational products.

Component 2: Products and Services   Reference: Chapter 4

List the products and services you will use this marketing plan to promote. Briefly describe each product or service.

Product/service	Description
Executive Coaching	*Help CEOs and senior executives improve their results by mastering systematic goal setting, accountability, and priorities. CEOs define the agenda; we help them implement.*
CFO for Rent®	*Take hands-on responsibility for a clearly defined and focused "mini-job description," often including directing full-time staff to achieve specific objectives.*
Executive Search	*Full-service retained search for CFO to controller positions, including helping clarify the role, qualifications, and compensation; completing the search; then structuring, presenting, and negotiating the offer.*
Executive Seminars	*Twelve-module series: Financial Management for Nonfinancial Executives. Designed and customized primarily for in-house presentation to management teams.*

Component 3: Target Market   Reference: Chapter 4

1. Market Description

Provide a general description of the primary market(s) you plan to target.
Include demographic and psychographic information as appropriate.

Will target CEOs in manufacturing, distribution, and service industries. Southern California will be the geographic focus for CFO for Rent® & Executive Search; Executive Coaching & Seminars will be nationwide. Will target companies with annual sales as follows:

Executive Coaching	*$1–$25 million*
CFO for Rent®	*$5–$50 million*
Executive Search	*$5–$100 million*
Executive Seminars	*$10–$100 million*

2. Targeted Prospects

List the names of the specific individuals and (if names are not known) organizations you will target. List as many as you can effectively manage.

Name	Company
1. *Gerald Shane*	*Qual-Pro Corporation*
2. *Jeff Lawrence*	*Trillium*
3. *James R. Swarthout*	*Samma Industries, Inc.*
4. *Robert M. Davidson*	*Davidson*
5. *Alexandra J. Rand*	*Internal & External Communications*
6. *Michael Feygin*	*Helisys*
7.	

Component 4: Competition   Reference: Chapter 4

1. Competitors

List and describe your primary competitors.

1. *Other financial management companies*
2. *Out-of-work CFOs*
3. *Certain CPA firms*
4.
5.

2. Unique Selling Position

How are you different from your primary competitors? Describe your unique competitive advantages.

Provide financial, technical, and business expertise. Teaching manner is unique. Offer superior communication skills and high degree of people sensitivity. Concept of CFO for Rent® provides a unique marketing advantage.

Component 5: Matching Needs and Prospective Sources   Reference: Chapter 11

List the types of help you need (see chapter 5) and the prospective information, support, and referral source(s) that might provide this help

Type of help (#)	Description	Prospective source(s)
2	*Distribute information*	*All*
4	*Invite me to attend events*	*All*
5	*Endorse my products and services*	*Mike, Bonnie, Joan*
6	*Nominate me for recognition & awards*	*John, Maryellen*
8	*Provide me with referrals*	*All*
9	*Make initial contact w/prospects, sources*	*All*
11	*Arrange a meeting on my behalf*	*David*
13	*Publish information for me*	*Mike, Joan, David*

Component 6: Tactics   Reference: Chapter 12

List the primary relationship development and referral marketing tactics you plan to use during the campaign. Briefly describe how each will be used.

Tactic #	Tactic name	Description of use
4	*Reporting*	*Will interview at least 3 of my sources for an article I will write on the major concerns of corporate executives*
7	*Advising*	*Will set up a tip of the week on answering/voice mail system*
8	*Announcing*	*Will provide information about upcoming events in newsletter*
12	*Inviting*	*Will invite each source to at least 2 of my keynoters*
15	*Collaborating*	*Will attempt to establish a collaboration with top 5 sources*
17	*Promoting*	*Will promote the services offered by my colleagues during meetings and in newsletter*

Component 7: Referral Marketing System

Reference: Chapters 13, 14, 17

1. Key Sources

List the names of the key sources you will focus on during the campaign. List as many as you can manage effectively.

1. *Mike Rounds*
2. *Joan Irvine*
3. *John Kinde*
4. *David Rohlander*
5. *Bonnie Dean*
6. *Maryellen Lipinski*
7.
8.
9.
10.

2. Briefing Your Sources

Describe the approaches you will use to brief your referral sources.

1. *One-on-one discussions first*
2. *Provide each source with a profile*
3. *Place each source on my newsletter mailing list*
4. *Send each source an invitation to our open house*
5.
6.

3. Rewarding and Recognizing Your Sources

Describe the methods you will use to recognize and reward your referral sources.

1. *Treat them to dinner at the Executive Club or restaurant of their choice*
2. *Provide a pair of complimentary tickets to a theater performance of their choice*
3. *Personal note of thanks*
4. *List and thank in the newsletter*
5.

Component 8: Time Budget

Reference: Chapter 18

Distribute by period the total time available for your campaign.

Period:	1	2	3	4	5	6	7	8	9	10	11	12	Total
	12	12	12	12	10	8	8	8	12	12	8	6	120

Component 9: Calendar   Reference: Chapter 18

List the major relationship development and referral marketing activities that will occur during your campaign.

Date	Activity
1997	
October	*Seminar*
	Quarterly newsletter
	Initiate monthly & bimonthly relationship development contacts
November	*Seminar*
December	*Host social event for sources*
	Include profile with holiday letter
1998	
January	*Seminar*
	Quarterly newsletter
February	*Seminar*
	Begin meeting with prospective sources one-on-one
March	*Seminar*
	Complete one-on-one meetings
April	*Seminar*
	Quarterly newsletter
	Open house for the new office
May	*Seminar*
	Assess effectiveness of referral marketing program
June	*Seminar*
July	*Quarterly newsletter*
August	*Seminar*
	Begin final evaluation of referral marketing program
	Begin planning for next referral marketing program
September	*Seminar*
	Complete final evaluation
	Complete referral marketing plan for next period

Component 10: Cost Budget   Reference: Chapter 18

Distribute by period the total funds available for your campaign.

Period: 1   2   3   4   5   6   7   8   9   10   11   12   Total

$ _240_ _240_ _240_ _240_ _200_ _160_ _160_ _160_ _240_ _240_ _160_ _120_ $_2400_

Component 11: Sales and Referral Projections   Reference: Chapter 19

List the products and services you plan to sell during your campaign. Perform the necessary calculations.

Product/ service	Unit price	No. units expected to be sold	Total projected sales	Expected sales from referrals	Expected % sales from referrals
1. _Executive Coaching_	$200/hr	500	$100,000	$70,000	70%
2. _CFO for Rent®_	$5,000/mo	10	$50,000	$35,000	70%
3. _Executive Search_	$2,000	10	$20,000	$20,000	100%
4. _Executive Seminars_	$3,000	10	$30,000	$25,000	83%
5.					
6.					

Total sales expected during 1st period: A. _$200,000_ B. _$150,000_

Expected % of total sales from referrals: C. _75%_

Component 12: Tracking and Evaluation   Reference: Chapter 20

List the tools and strategies that you will use to track, analyze, and evaluate the results of your referral marketing campaign. Include target dates for all actions.

Will complete a contact report following each scheduled contact with sources.
All referrals will be documented and tracked using the Business Referral Tool.

●

Glossary

business opportunity: any situation that has the potential to generate revenue for your business.

client: a prospect who has decided to purchase a product or service from you or otherwise provide you with a business opportunity; an individual who patronizes your business; a customer or patient.

competitive strategy: the business approaches and initiatives a company takes to attract customers, withstand competitive pressures, and strengthen its market position.

contact: a meeting, telephone conversation, letter, e-mail, or other communication between two or more individuals.

contact sphere: a group of businesses or professions that complement, rather than compete with, your business.

credibility: the second stage in the development of a relationship, the phase in which trust is established.

customer: client.

direct referral: a referral you receive from a source you pursued by taking specific actions.

GAINS: an acronym for the five kinds of information shared between partners in a developing business or personal relationship: goals, accomplishments, interests, networks, and skills.

Information Network: the component of your Network that consists of your most knowledgeable sources, the people who can provide you with the information and expertise you need to run a successful business.

management team: the leaders and decision makers of a business or other organization, each of whom has specific areas of expertise and responsibilities, such as finance, marketing, law, or personnel management.

Network: a diverse, balanced, and powerful system of sources — people from all facets of the business world — that will provide the information, support, and referrals you need to run a successful word-of-mouth business; with a capital *N*, the system of referral sources that you are endeavoring to set up in order to generate business and business opportunities by word of mouth.

profitability: the third phase of a developing relationship, in which prospects become customers and prospective sources provide business opportunities and referrals.

prospect: a potential buyer of your product or service.

reference period: a base period against which the results of a like period of your Referral Marketing Campaign are measured.

referral: a potential customer with whom you have a relationship initiated by a third party, or a business opportunity initiated by a third party.

referral gap: the extent to which a businessperson's desired referral business falls short of actual referral business.

Referral Network: the component of your Network consisting of individuals who help you generate new business by giving you the names of prospective clients and helping you contact them.

referral marketing: the practice of building a base of customers, clients, or patients by obtaining support from specific sources; the systematic cultivation of business by referrals.

Referral Marketing Campaign (RMC): a purposeful set of actions taken to increase business received through referrals.

Referral Marketing Plan: the written record of information, intentions, schedules, and budgets by which a Referral Marketing Campaign is implemented.

relationship development: the practice of establishing an acquaintanceship and cultivating from it a trusting friendship and a lasting professional association.

source: a person who identifies, brings to your attention, or sends you prospects you may convert to customers or business opportunities.

Support Network: the component of your Network that consists of people who respect and admire you and who can help your business at crucial times by encouraging you, working for you, filling in for you, or lending you money in an emergency.

VCP: visibility, credibility, and profitability — the three stages of a maturing vendor-customer or vendor-source relationship.

vendor: the person who is seeking and expecting to obtain referrals — that is, you.

visibility: the first stage in the development of a relationship, during which two individuals become aware of each other and begin to communicate and establish links.

BIBLIOGRAPHY

Baber, Anne, and Lynn Waymon. *Great Connections.* Manassas Park, Virginia: Impact Publications, 1992.

Boe, Anne. *Networking Success.* Encinitas, California: Seaside Press, 1994.

Boe, Anne, and Bette B. Youngs. *Is Your "Net" Working?* New York: John Wiley & Sons, 1989.

Burg, Bob. *Endless Referrals: Network Your Everyday Contacts into Sales.* New York: McGraw-Hill, 1994.

Cashman, Kevin J. *Networking: Building Relationships, Building Success.* St. Paul, Minnesota: Devine Multi-Media Publishing, 1994.

Cates, Bill. *Unlimited Referrals.* Wheaton, Maryland: Thunder Hill Press, 1996.

Davis, Robert. *Implement Now, Perfect Later: 52 Practical Ways to Increase Gains and Decrease Pains of Perfectionism.* Riverside, California: Robert Davis Associates, 1997.

Davis, Robert, and Laura Miller. *Total Quality Introductions* (audio-cassette). Upland, California: Robert Davis Associates, 1991.

Edwards, Paul, Sarah Edwards, and Laura Douglas. *Getting Business to Come to You.* Los Angeles: Jeremy P. Tarcher, 1991.

Fisher, Donna. *People Power: 12 Power Principles to Enrich Your Business, Career & Personal Networks.* Austin: Bard Press, 1995.

Fisher, Donna, and Sandy Vilas. *Power Networking: 55 Secrets for Personal & Professional Success.* Austin: MountainHarbour Publications, 1992.

Jolley, Willie. *It Only Takes a Minute to Change Your Life*. New York: St. Martin's Press, 1997.

Krannich, Robert L., and Caryl Rae Krannich. *Network Your Way to Job and Career Success*. Alexandria, Virginia: Impact Publications, 1989.

Mackay, Harvey. *Dig Your Well Before You're Thirsty*. New York: Doubleday, 1997.

Mackay, Harvey. *Swim with the Sharks Without Being Eaten Alive: Outsell, Outmanage, Outmotivate, and Outnegotiate Your Competition*. New York: William Morrow and Co., 1988.

Misner, Ivan R. *The World's Best Known Marketing Secret: Building Your Business with Word-of-Mouth Marketing*. Austin: Bard Press, 1994.

Misner, Ivan R. *Seven Second Marketing: How to Use Memory Hooks to Make You Instantly Stand Out in a Crowd*. Austin: Bard Press, 1996.

Naisbitt, John. *Megatrends: Ten New Directions Transforming Our Lives*. New York: Warner Books, 1982.

RoAne, Susan. *How to Work a Room*. New York: Warner Books, 1991.

RoAne, Susan. *The Secrets of Savvy Networking*. New York: Warner Books, 1993.

Sabah, Joe. *How to Get on Talk Show Radio All Across America* (audiotape). Denver: Pacesetter Publications, 1995.

Sheer, Mark. *Referrals*. Mission Viejo, California: Sheer Seminars, 1993.

Sukenik, Ron. *Networking Your Way to Success*. Dubuque, Iowa: Kendall/Hunt Publishing Co., 1995.

Thompson, Arthur, and A. J. Strickland. *Strategic Management: Concepts and Cases* (8th edition). Chicago: Irwin, 1995.

Wilson, Jerry R. *Word-of-Mouth Marketing*. New York: John Wiley & Sons, 1991.

INDEX

ABOUT BUSINESS NETWORK INT'L.

Business Network Int'l. (BNI) was founded by Dr. Ivan Misner in 1985 as a way for businesspeople to generate referrals in a structured, professional environment. BNI is now the largest referral networking organization of its kind in the world, with 70,000 members in more than 3,500 chapters spread acrsoss 18 countries. BNI members have generated millions of referrals worth over a billion dollars in business for the participants.

The primary purpose of the organization is to pass qualified business referrals to its members. Its mission is to teach business professionals that the word-of-mouth process is more about farming than it is about hunting: it's about the cultivation of professional relationships in a structured business environment for the mutual benefit of all. BNI's philosophy may be summed up in two words: "Givers gain." If you give business to people, you will get business from them.

BNI allows only one person per profession to join a chapter. The program is designed to allow businesspeople to develop long-term relationships, thereby creating a basis for trust and, inevitably, referrals.

To get more information on a chapter in your area, call 1-800-688-9394 or visit BNI's home page at www.bni.com.

●

About the National Speakers Association

The National Speakers Association is the only professional speakers' association in the world. It was founded in 1973 by the late Cavett Robert, CSP, CPAE, to promote educational opportunities, professionalism, and fellowship among professional speakers, as well as to raise the integrity and visibility of the speaking profession. The organization, which now has over 3,700 members in more than 35 chapters, is composed of experienced, developing, and aspiring professional speakers, as well as individuals who serve the profession with products and services, such as speakers' bureaus, rally producers, public relations agents, audiotape and video producers, and brochure specialists.

To get more information on a chapter in your area, call (602) 968-2552 or visit NSA's home page at www.nsaspeaker.org.